Dawning After Darkness

By Tim Ellison

Table of Contents

This book is written in dedication to my grandparents, William and Dolores Craft (Biba and Poppy)

Although you can't physically read this book, I'm sure it will reach you both in some way. The two of you have helped me to become person I am today, and without you, I can't imagine how I'd get to this point in my life. You will live forever in my heart.

Acknowledgements

My Mother, Cherie Craft:
Mom, without you, there is no me. Thank you for giving me the strength I needed to get this book done and published.

Michelle Prive:
The occasional missed appointments and ignored emails along this journey don't say it, so I'll say it here, you have been such an integral and essential part in this whole process and to thank you for making this book possible wouldn't be enough. I thank you not only for helping with the book, but for saving my life. I genuinely believe that without you, I may not have been around to even write this book.

Ms. Betty Bardige:
Thank you so much for all your help and support with this book. Without your help, this book would not have possible and I wouldn't have had the opportunity to touch so many lives. I have you to thank deeply, for this accomplishment.

Ms. Margaret McPartland:
Thank you for pulling me out of what may have been my worst rut, yet. You may not know this, but when you decided to help me with this project, I was in a really bad place. Your assistance gave me the strength I needed to finish this book. For that, I am so grateful.

For All of my Brothers:
I know we don't always sit down and talk about our feelings or what we're dealing with, but I want to let you all know that you have all saved my life, with your efforts to help me get back to myself. Whether it was watching sports or building a business together, each one of you have played a huge part in my recovery. We may not all share the same parents but blood could not make any of us any closer, and you all know who you are.

Introduction

"If you break your leg, you are going to go to the doctor to get that leg healed. If something inside of you feels like it's wounded, it's just like a physical injury. You got to go get help. There's nothing weak about that. It's strong."
- President Obama

I can't believe I'm really doing this. After months of pressure from everyone around me, and my spirits getting worse, I finally gave in. Everyone told me this would help me so much and that it was the first step towards the end of this battle but I didn't want to hear it. I've never been one who was easily convinced by anyone to do anything so this had to be my choice. Here I am, sitting in this waiting room with my mom Cherie, my head full of questions. Constantly asking myself how I got here and wondering how this would help me at all. I never thought I could get this low, feel this defeated. How was talking to someone going to help me get through this? Therapy was something I tried before, but after the first experience didn't go well, I never returned. I can look back on it now and say that I was too young to really digest what was being offered to me by the therapist and the whole idea was just too much for me at the time.

I've been in and out of the hospital so many times for medical issues, that Boston Medical Center feels like more of a second home for me, but this time was different. There was a nervous feeling I couldn't get over, butterflies I couldn't lose, as if it was my first time there. My mom kept catching my eye, smiling, winking and even gently holding my hand, but those things didn't provide the comfort that they usually do. The woman we were waiting to see couldn't come out fast enough. I felt like everyone in the room was staring at me. Being twenty-one in the Pediatric waiting room can be awkward in any case.

Finally, a woman comes out and calls for my mom and I to follow her back to her office. Seeing that the last therapist I saw was a man and the one before that was an older woman, it took me by surprise to see that my therapist was a younger woman. She couldn't have been much older than maybe 30 years old. She was a thin brunette, who appeared young and soft spoken, but somehow wise, beyond her years. She introduced herself as Michelle and invited us back into her office. The walk felt like it went on for hours, as the questions and worries started to pile up again while I contemplated everything that was going to happen during my first appointment. I wasn't expecting to say much, and seeing that my mom was there, I knew I wouldn't have to.

When we got into the room the first thing I noticed was how cold it was in there. I was looking for some comfort and I couldn't find it, even with all the cliché depression posters on the wall, like "Symptoms of Depression", or the ones with the 1-800 hotline numbers, nothing was working for me. The introduction portion felt much like an interview, obviously not your average interview, though. The questions started piling on, one on top of another, causing me to dig back far into my memory for the answers. Most of them were questions that I'd already heard one hundred times already, but some were new. Those are the ones that stood out to me. As the questions got more personal, I started getting more intrigued by what felt like just another conversation, not a therapy session. These weren't questions I could just breeze through and give routine answers to; here I really had to think. For the first time in a very long time, I was doing something that actually felt therapeutic for me. While answering Michelle's questions, I also started simultaneously answering questions of my own that I had for myself, like *"Is this all in my head?"* The

6

answer being, *"No, this isn't just my imagination. Yes, I am really depressed and it is a serious illness!"*

This wasn't going at all how I thought it would, it was a lot better! I had first imagined myself sitting there as my mom talked to my new therapist while I sat and listened for the most part. Maybe I'd have to nod or shake my head a few times if I was needed, but I thought I would sit back as my mom took control. She knows me so well and wants what's best for me so I felt comfortable with her leading the way.

Anyone who knows my mom, Cherie Craft, can understand why I felt comfortable letting her take the lead. She has a big heart and smiles easily; that smile instantly conveys the love, care and concern she has for the lucky subject of her attention. She is a social worker/counselor/advocate by training and by nature, but you'd be foolish to let her soft heart fool you. Degrees, accolades and honors aside, she is a fierce protector of all she holds dear and her love of her children, rivals that of any ferocious mama bear. She's raised five of us, including four of us who are now adults, my cousins, and my baby sister Alani, who is just four years old, but hundreds over the years have referred to her as "Mom". All in her orbit, family, friends, employees, and families she's worked with, all know that there is something special in the way she cares for all of us, and we all feel extremely grateful.

Despite what I anticipated would happen, the plan to have my mom take the lead was not at all how it went. There I was, spilling out the details of some of the hardest times of my life to a complete stranger. Just recently I had told myself I was done communicating with people for the most part. I was starting to feel like no matter what I said, there was no resolution to my problem. I had expressed myself before, completely opened up, only to continue to feel the same way as before. This is why when the idea of therapy

7

was brought up, I was always quick to shoot it down. I was told there were only two ways to treat depression, one was by going through some sort of therapy, and the other involved taking prescription medication for it.

The idea of taking medicine was always a no go for me. For some reason, it made me feel like I was so different from everyone around me. Nobody else was taking meds for what they were going through, at least not that I knew of, and that was a part of the reason why I was so against it. I heard a few people say taking the meds made them worse in different ways, and others say it just didn't work. The doctors of course were trying to sway me into taking them. I never really even sat down and thought to myself about the possibility of taking meds for something other than physical injuries. I would say it was just the overall bad stigma about the idea that led me to turn my nose up at it. Seeing that I was being so stubborn about the idea of taking meds, and I felt like I had to make a decision of some sort, I decided to allow my doctor and my mom to hook me up with a therapist, instead.

My experience there was a lot different than what I had anticipated though. I was able to just sit back and reflect on all the things that were causing me to stress so heavily. Michelle used different methods and exercises that helped me sort my thoughts out for once in a very long time. Sometimes when you're depressed, you forget what you were even sad about in the first place and fall into something a lot deeper. It's a tough place to explain but I'd suffice it to say your thoughts get all foggy and compiled into one huge emotion, and it completely kills your mood. You just become totally shut down with no explanation for anyone. You can't express what's wrong because you don't even know anymore. You crawl into a shell and don't have the energy or motivation to talk to anyone anymore because you see no point. For a while, that's exactly where

I was. I wasn't really open to any suggestions anyone had and continuously shot down ideas for treatment from those around me. I felt like there was no quick solution and hoped that it was something that would just go away. But in just my first session, for the first time in as long as I could remember, I was starting to figure out why I was so sad again.

Michelle, allowed me to separate my issues into different categories and then helped me make a plan on how to attack these issues. Some of them carried more weight than others, some were almost impossible to completely solve. It was a process of prioritizing for me. What were the things that triggered my depression the most? Once I figured out which of my stressors I was going to tackle first, I felt more sense of direction. Leaving that office, again I was feeling a lot different then I originally thought I would. I was anticipating leaving the hospital feeling exactly the same as when I first arrived, maybe even a little more annoyed than before. Instead, I actually felt like I had a direction to follow. Talking to my therapist allowed me to make goals for myself. Those foggy thoughts were starting to become clearer for me.

Chapter 1
The Backstory: A Storm Brewing for Years

"It was beginning to get fuzzy – I couldn't even tell which day or which city I was at….. My mother was very persistent and she kept saying that I had to take care of my mental health." - Beyonce

One scary part about life is that you can be developing something detrimental to your health without even noticing. That's how depression crept up on me, and infiltrated my life.

I grew up in inner city Boston, and was bused to school in the affluent suburb of Brookline. Overall, I had a great childhood. I was a normal, fun loving, energetic and naturally curious kid. I had some early health challenges that resulted in a few hospitalizations, as young as a year old, but nothing that indicated the health challenges that were to come later in life. My three siblings and I were raised by a single mom, but we never wanted for anything. She worked hard, and although we spent much of our free time at our grandparents' house in the housing project where my mom grew up, we lived in our own, single family home. We had a village of close family and friends to share great times with and to help to raise us right. My grandparents, Biba and Poppy, along with aunts, uncles, cousins, and family friends who were just as much a part of our family, were a part of our everyday life, and formed a strong loving and supportive team.

I was the youngest in my home growing up, with two older sisters, Christian and Keya, along with my older brother Darius. We are each about a year apart, in age, but Christian was always like a second mother to us, and just as we did as children, we all still share a special bond.

We spent so much of our childhood enjoying life within our "village". As children, we had great times in the housing project where our mom was raised and most of our family lived. We would play street ball, hide and seek, and turn on the fire hydrants when the weather was unbearably hot. Often times, we would pile into cars to go to the beach, bowling alley or an amusement park. Mostly we would just hang out, adults and children, in someone's house or front yard, laughing, talking listening to music, sharing meals, stories, celebrating good times and supporting each other when trouble arose.

At home, we would run and chase each other through our big, old, single family house, have big cookouts in the backyard with family and friends, engage snow ball fights during those harsh New England winters and water gun battles (usually the boys against the girls), when we enjoyed our short, precious summers. We would all sit out, late into the night on our huge front porch, swinging on the swing or sitting on the stairs playing Uno or Monopoly. Once or twice a year, we would go on an amazing vacation – to Disney World, Hershey Park, or a quick weekend getaway to New York City. Once we even went to the Bahamas, which was amazing. We didn't have a lot of money, but we never knew that. Life was good, and we were happy.

Throughout my childhood and coming of age, however, I went through a number of challenging times that I'm sure contributed to me eventually suffering from depression. From the illnesses I mentioned, to losses of loved ones, and other traumatic events, it was probably building all along, but life just seemed to go along, and after each incident, I seemed to be okay.

The illnesses started when I was just a year old. I always seemed to come down with the strangest diagnosis. Pneumococcal Bacteremia at 15 months; Kawasaki's Disease when I was three. Yes, Kawasaki – and no, it has nothing to do with the motorcycle brand, it was a communicable disease that looks like Scarlett Fever on the outside, but internally, attacks the valves and arteries around the heart; Viral infection at five; pneumonia and the flu at 9, and all required lengthy hospitalizations. The worse was at 13, when I was hospitalized for months. That's how I became so comfortable at Boston Medical Center. It was my second home. I had dozens of appointments and visited so many specialty units, I became somewhat of a celebrity there! The staff were all so nice and welcoming, I always felt well cared for, even when I was feeling my worst. Every time I suffered an illness, I was wrapped in love and support from our large network, and came through fully recovered.

Each time, after an illness or incident, my pediatrician and my mom thought I should see someone like a therapist or counselor, and a couple of times, when I was small, I actually went, but it didn't seem helpful at all, as far as I could remember, so I never saw it as a valuable use of my time.

I had a great number of friends at school and in my neighborhood, so I was a very social kid who was outgoing and had close relationships with a lot of people. Even as a kid, I had a large network of people around me so I never felt alone. I was a pretty good student, and excelled in my academic work. I was always outspoken and opinionated and was seen as a leader among my friends both at school and in my neighborhood. I was kind, respectful and humble, but self-assured as a kid, and never had any issues with my self-esteem, until my battle with depression began.

Like many people growing up around me, my passion was basketball. Aside from my family, from as long as I can remember, it was the greatest love of my life. I didn't want anything more than to be a professional basketball player and despite some early occasional health issues, I worked hard every day so one day I'd maybe have that opportunity. I was good – great at it, and won several trophies and tournaments to prove it. I began playing on a team at the Dorchester YMCA right after my 5th birthday, but I had been playing around the house since I could remember. Every day of my life I practiced, drilled, played in leagues and tournaments, studied my craft, read books, watched videos, went to camps, and more. Basketball was as essential to me as air and water. However, at 14 after a series of hospitalizations, and complications, that dream died, and while I was entering into the difficult stage of adolescence. I'd lost my first love - basketball, and didn't know how to cope with that. While it might sound trivial, and my breakdown didn't actually occur until my third year in college, I honestly believe that that was the beginning of my battle with depression. I never felt the same about myself, after my hoop dreams died.

Chapter 2
On Campus with Depression

"I was scared and depressed for a while. Not that I had any f-ing reason to be depressed – I mean, I was going to college and everything. It was not like I was hungry." Joseph Gordon-Levitt, star actor, 3rd Rock from the Sun.

Going to school with depression is nearly impossible. When I first started college, I felt like my life was going in the right direction for sure. I was clear that I wanted to study business, because my goal was to be an entrepreneur, and to start a number of lucrative businesses, in real estate music and technology.

In high school, I made sure that the college that I chose had a few essential elements. One of those was that it had to be a reasonable distance from home, but not so far that I couldn't get back by myself. Another was that I had to have a few of my friends at the school with me so I could ensure that I was comfortable there. It also had to have a strong business program, with lots of opportunities to explore entrepreneurship. Adding in those factors to a couple others, like nice dorms and decent food, I chose UMass Dartmouth. Two of my closest friends from elementary, middle and high school, the twins, Devon and Dashawn were also going to UMass D, and we shared a triple dorm room freshman year.

My first year at UMass D went by fast, but we had a good time and maintained good grades as well so everything was going as planned. By sophomore year we really got the living by yourself experience when we moved to the

Dells. The Dells at UMass Dartmouth are like mini town houses so you feel like you have your own apartment with an upstairs and downstairs, kitchen, living room and everyone has their own bedroom. That year, I met many new people and built even more friendships along the way. I set up my schedule so that I could wake up around ten or eleven every morning and be done by about three in the afternoon every day.

I was studying business and I enjoyed the classes that pertained to my major, like Intro to Business, and even the writing classes, but the ones that didn't seem relevant usually weren't so fun, like micro and macro-Economics (Ugh). In our free time, my friends and I would get together and play basketball in the gym or participate in the intermural basketball leagues that the school offered and enjoyed each other's company playing video games. Something that has always been important to me is making sure that I maintain strong relationships with the people that I am close to and I was able to build a stronger bond with Devon and Dashawn, as well as others while I was up at Dartmouth.

Junior year, however, was a tough one for me. Everything had felt differently and I wasn't sure if I could go back. In retrospect, this is when the depression started to hit me. All summer, before junior year began, I had battled back and forth in my head about whether or not I wanted to return to school that coming year.

Part of me wanted to stay home and work on my business ventures. I was trying to get my laptop and phone repair company "Tech Bros" off the ground, and I knew going back to school would take away from progress. Another couple of my childhood friends, Obi and Oshun started Tech Bros. with me, and we were just getting things in order, developing our business plan and launching

15

services. I was feeling uneasy about my finances, and while my mom gave me allowance and I worked over the summer and part-time, when I could, I still needed to make extra money on the side. I knew that Tech Bros. had the potential to take off and to provide the financial security I sought, if I could only devote enough time to it.

That, along with the fact that I was not feeling entirely like myself, added to the reluctance I felt about going back to school. Honestly, I probably should've mentioned how I was feeling to my mother, but I knew how important it was to her that we all finish our education, and she was so proud of me. I didn't want to disappoint her, so I convinced myself that I would get over my reservations and settle in once I got back on campus. Unfortunately, that was not how things turned out.

When I went back for junior year, the battle was tougher than I anticipated. For starters, our dorm situation wasn't what we thought it would be. It took a turn for the worse and we didn't get a Dell townhouse for junior year like we thought we would. Instead, we were back in the single room dorms, and very unhappy about it. It made things more uncomfortable for me, and I felt almost claustrophobic in my tiny room. My depression at that point, although I had yet to realize it, was worsening at a rapid pace.

The battle of waking up every morning having to go to class is hard enough. Mix in depression, diagnosed or not, and you have a mental war on your hands. The getting out of bed part gets ten times harder than usual, and you find yourself buried in homework. The idea of eating is so stressful that most times you choose to eat nothing, because it involves you doing less. Depression is a major motivation killer, and to make it through school, you need a ton of motivation and determination. I didn't really know that I was depressed at the time, but I knew something was terribly wrong. I had always been a go-getter and strived for excellence. As an athlete, winning or at least giving my all, was part of my DNA, but I found myself caring less and less.

You start to think of everything in a negative light when you suffer from depression and it started forcing me to look at college very differently. I started questioning whether it was the right option for me and doubted my ability to succeed there. That's when school became a nightmare for me. The lack of motivation hit me hard, and going to class was getting to be a harder task by the day.

According to the American Psychological Association's September 2011 article by Arielle Eiser,
entitled *"Crisis on Campus"*:
"The 2010 National Survey of Counseling Center Directors (NSCCD) found that 44 percent of counseling center clients had severe psychological problems, a sharp increase from 16 percent in 2000. The most common of these disorders were depression, anxiety, suicidal ideation, alcohol abuse, eating disorders and self-injury. A 2010 survey of students by the American College Health Association found that 45.6 percent of students surveyed reported feeling hopeless, and 30.7 percent reported feeling so depressed that it was difficult to function during the past 12 months.

While depression and anxiety consistently rank as the most common mental disorders treated at college counseling centers, an often overlooked but equally serious problem is the rising number of students struggling with eating disorders, substance abuse and self-injury. The NSCCD study found that 24.3 percent of college counseling center directors have noticed more clients with eating disorders, 39.4 percent have noted an increased number of clients suffering from self-injury issues and 45.7 percent have reported an increased number of clients struggling with alcohol abuse.

As grim as these statistics are, however, these percentages are probably even higher since students with substance abuse and eating disorders are less likely to seek treatment at counseling centers than students with depression and anxiety disorders."

Having depression is a lot to deal with by itself, when you add anxiety to the mix, it becomes a second war you feel like you have to fight by yourself. The anxiety would keep me up for a lot of the night and those previously long nights of sleep got shorter and shorter for me. I had planned my schedule a certain way so that despite how long I stayed up, I would still get my fair share of sleep. Having depression and anxiety makes it extremely hard to maintain your normal schedule, especially your sleep schedule.

I would stay up all night stressing over every small detail all of my entire day and stressing even harder over what would happen tomorrow. If I had a test, I would sit up for hours telling myself I was going to fail and would stare at my laptop without any productivity because the thought of taking a test became even more terrifying than usual. If I had a big assignment due, I would be up trying to piece together a long-term project over one night's time (I'm sure we've all been there though) because I lacked the motivation I used to have to get things done on time.

One thing I always made sure I did during all my days at school was to stay up to date with my homework. That's a work ethic I'd committed to back in elementary school, and kept up throughout my entire school career. No matter how I was doing otherwise in any class, my homework completion was always on point. I was never too confident with test taking, so I wanted to make sure there was one area I could always count on doing well in. I'd never slipped with homework before, so when I stopped caring about doing it, I knew I had a problem. I stopped paying close attention to when things were due, and it felt like projects and papers were multiplying. Procrastination is something I believe most students go through to some degree, but for me, it went from procrastination to not doing anything at all. I would tell myself every day, multiple times a day, that I would start or finish a project or assignment and most of the time, I would leave class and go straight to sleep. All I wanted to do after a while was sleep.

Everything that used to interest me became less fun and started feeling more like a job to me. I was overanalyzing everything, and it led to isolation. I would isolate myself from everyone and then be mad at my friends for feeling like they abandoned me. I would tell people I didn't want to be a part of something and then be mad because I wasn't included. It was a back and forth battle that I was having in my head, consistently over the span of each day. After a while I decided that being alone was better than being around people and having to pretend I was happy. At least when I was alone I could be sad in peace, I thought. I didn't want people asking questions about the changes they saw in me, and I could avoid all that by completely disconnecting myself from everything and everyone. If I managed to pry myself out of bed and make it to class, I would immediately go back to my dorm room and try to fall back asleep. I was miserable, lost weight from not eating, felt weak both physically and mentally, and completely disconnected from everyone.

After a few weeks went by feeling the same way I started strongly considering leaving school. The very idea of taking a break from school was something I'd never really considered before, but due to my mental state at the time, it started to feel like my only option. I knew I wouldn't be able to last the rest of the semester at the rate I was going and that idea led to even more stress. I was constantly having battles back and forth in my head, contemplating what my next step was. I found myself weighing my options and started thinking about the positives and negatives of both of leaving and going home, or trying to stay. School was like a safety net for me. I wasn't sure if college was going to actually help me do what I wanted to do with my life, but I felt like a long as I was in school I was on a positive path. It felt good to be in school and be able to tell people that I was in college studying business when they asked. Seeing that most of my friends were also in school, I felt like I was right where I was supposed to be. Taking all of that into consideration, plus the fact that I was concerned about disappointing my mom and everyone back at home, I felt obligated to stay in school.

Even though my heart was invested in the idea of being in school, my mind was on a different page. Not eating well, not sleeping, and the major lack of motivation I got from being depressed ultimately forced my hand in making the decision to depart from UMass D. When I finally talked to my mom about it, she was surprisingly supportive, after I told her how I had been suffering. She surprised me at first, but honestly my mom has always been so supportive and concerned about my overall well-being, I should've known that she would support my decision and be ready and willing to help.

Once we made it official, I didn't know how to feel. Part of me felt relieved because deep down, I knew it was the only choice for me at the time. There was no way I would've been able to stay at school and continue to be productive while I was dealing with my depression. Part of me felt disappointed because I'd always finished what I'd started.

Even though I knew that I was making the right decision, somehow, I still felt down about it.

I struggled with the thought of having to tell people I was leaving and the thought of explaining it to them was something that kept me up numerous nights. I knew everyone would be confused because I did such a good job of hiding my feelings so no one really knew the magnitude of what I was going through. I knew people would have questions; I sat and thought about what people would ask and what I would say. I convinced myself that I would be back to school that year one way or another so that's what I told people when they asked. Everyone tried to convince me to stay in college, which of course made everything harder than it already was. It made me start to question my decision even more and that was a burden that I couldn't handle. Luckily enough, my friends who knew me so well understood that going home gave me an opportunity to hit the reset button and figure out how I was going to get better.

UMass D, like most colleges, offers a medical leave of absence and my mom and I chose to go down that route. It allowed me to leave school indefinitely until I felt like I was ready to come back. We had to meet with a school counselor and provide documentation from a medical provider, and once those requirements were met, I was all set.

Moving my stuff out of school had to be one of the hardest things I've had to do in a while. I was going home to a lot of questions. I didn't know how I was going to get better and wasn't sure if going home was even going to help me, but now it was too late to turn back. My college roommates were also two of my closest childhood friends. Leaving some of the closest people to me without a real explanation was tougher than I can really explain, but I'll just say it was something that you could never prepare yourself for. It felt like everything was happening so fast, like the sky was falling and there was nothing anyone could do to stop it.

I drove back home by myself and I can remember having a long conversation on the phone with my mom. I was freaking out because the fact that I was leaving school finally set in and became a reality for me. It caused me to start questioning who I was and what I was going to be. When I finally got home and moved all of my stuff back in, it felt like I was starting a new chapter. This was supposed to be the beginning of my recovery, and I had a long way to go.

I started doing some research on depression while I was home and from school. I was alarmed to discover that several studies focusing on Black college students and mental health have found that there is a significant number of Black young men in college committing suicide. *According to the Centers for Disease Control and Prevention, suicide is the third leading cause of death among young black men ages 16-24.* - Psychiatry.org, *Depression and Suicide Among Black Men in College,* May 31, 2016.

I obviously didn't know it at the time, but taking a leave of absence from school to deal with my depression honestly may have saved my life.

Chapter 3
The Bad Stigma of Depression

"The next generation must grow up knowing that mental health is a key component of overall health and there is no shame, stigma or barriers to seeking out care." - Secretary of State Hillary Clinton

The stigma around mental health and mental health treatment continues to prevent many struggling with depression from getting the help that they need. Many studies have found that men are a lot less likely to get help for depression than women are. Most men have issues coming to terms with mental illness overall, and I found myself right there with the majority of my peers.

In the National Institute of Mental Health publication, Men and Depression, this topic is explored. "Many men do not recognize, acknowledge, or seek help for depression. They may be reluctant to talk about how they are feeling."

I had issues, but didn't want people to know I had them. I've always considered myself a strong-minded person who couldn't care less what people say or think, but this issue was contradicting my whole existence. I found myself obsessing over how I would be perceived if people found out I had depression, never mind that I was taking something daily to help treat it. There's no way I would separate myself from everyone I know in that way. I thought that taking the meds would make me so different from everyone else and it killed me inside. The idea of having to take something every day because I couldn't control what was going on in my head was something I couldn't deal with. My overall feelings were that everybody goes through things and most people get through it without having to take medication.

I asked a few people close to me about medication and I didn't hear anything positive, and that, in no way, helped the cause. I heard things about the side effects that concerned and scared me out of it (even though I had already done a good job of talking myself out anyway). I also talked to a few people who told me that they had clinical depression but never took any meds for it at all. They told me that the medicine didn't work, and they had found other ways to cope with how they were feeling. So, at this point not only had I built my own negative feelings towards the medicine, but unknowingly, a few people swayed me away from the idea of it as well.

Another aspect of the stigma involving taking medicine and getting help for depression with men, is this sense of being "macho" that we have. I think most of us feel like it makes us less of a man to seek help for mental illness. Most of us are in situations where we have to be the man of the house, even starting at a young age, and that makes us feel like we have to carry all of our burdens on our own shoulders. We rarely open up and talk about our issues in the first place, never mind actually going to talk to someone about what we're going through or take medication for it. In a lot of cases, the man in the family carries a ton of pressure on his shoulders and the main perception of depression is that we don't have time to be sad because we have too much to take care of.

What helped me ultimately, aside from reaching the end of my rope, was discovering that so many people that I admire, struggle with trauma, depression and/or anxiety, as well. Some of them are quoted in the chapters, but here is a more complete list, over 40 in total, although I'm sure there are others:

24

Abraham Lincoln, 16th President
Chris Evans, Actor (Captain America)
Kevin Love, NBA Superstar
Jay Z, Music Mogul, Rap Star
Kendrick Lamar, Musical Superstar
Beyonce, Musical Superstar
Maurice Bernard, Actor (Sonny, General Hospital)
Adele, Musical Superstar
Brian Dawkins, NFL Hall of Famer
Demar DeRozen, NBA Superstar
Elon Musk, Billionaire Inventor
Kanye West, Musical Superstar Rap Artist
Steve Smith, NFL Superstar
Kid Cudi, Musical Superstar, Rap Artist
Eminem, Musical Superstar, Rap Artist
Dwayne "The Rock" Johnson, Athlete/Actor
Russell Brand, Actor
Miley Cyrus, Singer
Brandon Marshall, NFL Star
Ryan Phillippe, Actor
Mark Twain, Author/Writer
Terry Bradshaw, NFL Hall of Famer
Brad Pitt, Oscar Winner Actor
Angelina Jolie, Actress, Oscar Winner Actor
Lady Gaga, Musical Superstar
Jim Carrey, Actor
Ellen DeGeneres, Actress/ Emmy Winning Talk Show Host
Michael Phelps, Olympic Gold Winning Swimmer
Reese Witherspoon, Actress
Uma Thurman, Actress
Channing Tatum, Actor
Halle Berry, Oscar Winning Actress
Princess Diana, Princess of Wales
Prince Harry, Prince of Wales
Alicia Keys, Grammy Winning Singer
Demi Lovato, Grammy Winning Singer

DMX, Rap star/Actor
Oscar de la Hoya, Champion Boxer
Jerry West, NBA Hall of Famer
Johnny Depp, Oscar Winning Actor
Sheryl Crow, Grammy Winning Singer
Trevor Noah, Host, The Daily Show
Mike Tyson, Champion Boxer
JK Rowling, Award Winning Author
Kerry Washington, Emmy Winning Actress

The list goes on, but I'm sure you get the picture – mental illness strikes scores of people, and excludes no one based on gender, race, color or creed; it doesn't matter if you are rich, famous, brilliant or powerful. These celebrities, athletes, business tycoons and politicians have been brave enough to share their stories, fighting stigma and giving others the courage to do the same. I am grateful to them for sharing their battles, and am proud to join their ranks.

Chapter 4
The Reality of Depression

"I could put all my opponents in the ring, and battle all of them, but this monster is going to be the toughest fight of my life." – Oscar De La Hoya, Olympic Gold Medal & Professional Boxer

One thing about depression that everyone who suffers from it comes to terms with at some point is that you can't control it. It isn't something you can just turn on and off and I believe that may be the hardest concept for us men to understand. We love being in control and feeling like we know what's going on, especially when it comes to ourselves. Depression totally rips away your control of your own mind. It takes you places you never thought you could go, male or female, that's not something you get over on your own.

Another issue we don't initially consider is how deeply the way that people see you can have a major impact on the way you see yourself and the decisions you make. Far more than you realize. As I mentioned earlier, depression forced me to start thinking about how everyone else looked at me and felt about me. It took away a lot of the confidence I had in myself. I'm sure that is also a huge factor that adds to the stigma that prevents us from seeking and receiving help.

Most people, especially men, feel like having depression makes them weak in the first place. It's something you feel like you need to hide from people, like a deep dark secret you have. Even though it's completely normal to go through it, our society doesn't feel comfortable letting others know about what it is that we're struggling with. Naturally, nobody wants anyone to know their struggle because it makes them feel exposed and also gives people the power to judge them. In the back of my head, I had already convinced myself that I was going to somehow get through this on my own and I wouldn't need a therapist or medication to assist me. After coming home and visiting my lifelong pediatrician and voicing how I felt about the ideas of therapy or medication, Dr. Siegel brought something to my attention. Those weren't just two random options among many, they were the only options. Me being stubborn, I told my doctor that I wasn't interested in either and I would see if I got better on my own. Seeing that he obviously couldn't force me to and I was so adamant about not wanting help, Dr. Siegel, who had cared for me since birth, told me there was nothing else he could do and I left the hospital even more confused.

Chapter 5
Being Sad vs. Being Depressed

"Sad hurts but it's a healthy feeling. It is a necessary thing to feel. Depression is very different." – J.K. Rowling, author of world renowned Harry Potter series

Telling people that you have depression can be hard for all kinds of reasons. One of those reasons is because if you don't suffer from depression, you can never fully understand it. A lot of people make the mistake of associating people who suffer from depression with the simple thought of just being sad. I've heard tons of people who are feeling sad say "I'm depressed" and they are the furthest thing from it. Feeling sad is an emotion, being depressed is an illness.

It's way deeper than just being sad at the moment and the desensitization of the term has forced some people to keep their depression to themselves. Being depressed is bad enough, it's even worse when you feel like people don't understand you. Understanding that I had support felt great, but I felt like I still hadn't found anyone who could really relate to what I was going through, and that made things even tougher.

I believe that part of the problem is that nowadays, we don't pay enough attention to what depression really is and how serious it should be taken. Depression is an illness and it should be taken as such. I don't think people would be so quick to label themselves as being depressed if they really knew what that entailed.

The National Institute of Health lists the following criteria to diagnose depression:

"Depression (major depressive disorder or clinical depression) is a common but serious mood disorder. It

causes severe symptoms that affect how you feel, think, and handle daily activities, such as sleeping, eating, or working. To be diagnosed with depression, the symptoms must be present for at least two weeks."

It goes on to say,

"If you have been experiencing some of the following signs and symptoms most of the day, nearly every day, for at least two weeks, you may be suffering from depression":

- *Persistent sad, anxious, or "empty" mood*
- *Feelings of hopelessness, or pessimism*
- *Irritability*
- *Feelings of guilt, worthlessness, or helplessness*
- *Loss of interest or pleasure in hobbies and activities*
- *Decreased energy or fatigue*
- *Moving or talking more slowly*
- *Feeling restless or having trouble sitting still*
- *Difficulty concentrating, remembering, or making decisions*
- *Difficulty sleeping, early-morning awakening, or oversleeping*
- *Appetite and/or weight changes*
- *Thoughts of death or suicide, or suicide attempts*
- *Aches or pains, headaches, cramps, or digestive problems without a clear physical cause and/or that do not ease even with treatment*

"Not everyone who is depressed experiences every symptom. Some people experience only a few symptoms while others may experience many. Several persistent symptoms in addition to low mood are required for a diagnosis of major depression, but people with only a few – but distressing – symptoms may benefit from treatment of their "subsyndromal" depression. The severity and frequency of symptoms and how long they last will vary

depending on the individual and his or her particular
illness. Symptoms may also vary depending on the stage
of the illness." National Institute of Health, Depression
Overview.
https://www.nimh.nih.gov/health/topics/depression/index.s
html

Chapter 6
The Moment of Truth: The Diagnosis

"I am not at peace. I haven't been since you've known me. If I didn't come here (in-patient treatment), I would've done something to myself. I simply am a damaged human swimming in a pool of emotions every day of my life. There's a ragin' violent storm inside of my life at all times. IDK what peace feels like IDK how to relax. My anxiety and depression have ruled my life for as long as I can remember ...." – Kid Cudi, Hip Hop Music Artist, after checking himself into rehab for depression.

When the notion that I was clinically depressed was introduced, hundreds of questions started circling in my head and just like that, I had no idea who I was. Dr. Siegel had been my primary care provider since birth, and had been leading my care team through many close calls with my physical health, so I trusted him with my life, but I was at a loss for words. There were so many questions I wanted to ask when he first informed me of the diagnosis, but no words came out. Being depressed is one thing, knowing that you suffer from "depression" is a completely different animal.

Dr. Siegel started giving different options for treatment, but at that point, I was no good. As soon as I heard the initial diagnoses, my body shut down. I was ready to leave the hospital and go straight home so I could shut everyone out. Being labeled with the diagnosis "major depressive disorder" was like being branded a leper. I wanted no part of it, and although I really wanted – needed - to get better, I didn't feel like anything was going to work. He was talking to me and I was looking right at him, but I heard nothing he was saying. All I could hear was the diagnosis being given, over and over in my head repeatedly. I couldn't be "that". I was Tim Ellison, strong, confident, a leader. I didn't want

32

to face the fact that I was suffering from a mental illness, but deep inside, I knew that I was and that I was eventually going to have to deal with it,

After I got over the initial shock of finding out I was suffering from depression, I tried to actually listen to what my Dr. Siegel was suggesting to me. He told me I basically had two options. The first was to start seeing a therapist, and the second involved taking some sort of medication. Once he started listing the names of the different medications and what they were used for, I stopped listening again. There was absolutely no way I was going to start taking medicine for something involving my mental health. Unfortunately, I was used to being at the hospital due to all the health challenges I'd had in the past, and I'd had to take medications for physical health diagnosis. So, the pill taking wasn't necessarily the issue for me, it was the stigma. I found myself in the same situation as most men in this country.

Chapter 7
Beginning Therapy

"I started therapy, which I still do today. I also see a nutritionist and I meditate. Learning how to love myself and my body is a lifelong process, but I definitely don't struggle the way I use to. Therapy helped me realize that maybe it's okay for me to express my feelings." - Kerry Washington, Actress and star of award winning series "Scandal"

For me, the decision between taking medicine or going to therapy was like choosing the lesser of two evils. I would constantly go back and forth, between which one I thought was more embarrassing and thought about which one of them had the worse stigma. The most important part of the decision was the one I was worried the least about, and that was which one would help me more effectively. After getting some advice and hearing people's previous experiences with both options, I decided to start going to therapy. This was one of the hardest decisions I've ever had to make and it was because deep down, I wasn't sure that either of these options would work for me. Everyone was pushing me so hard and I knew I was slipping so I felt like I had to choose something, but choosing therapy wasn't a decision I was too happy with, initially. I didn't think simply going in to talk to someone could actually help me. The question of how talking was going to cure my depression was one that I revisited on a consistent basis. I had tried therapy once before when I was younger for issues surrounding my dad and his absence in my life and I felt like it did nothing for me. I was pretty young so I couldn't remember what it was about the therapy that turned me off; maybe it was the therapist, or maybe it just wasn't right for me.

Those negative thoughts I was battling didn't really like the idea of therapy at all, either. I kept telling myself that it was going to be a waste of time. I would think about not wanting to have to share with someone all my personal business and feelings. I'm not someone who is extremely expressive to other people, especially people I don't know, so I was seriously thinking about how this was going to work for me. My mom, who I trust more than anyone else on this earth, continued to push the idea of therapy and insisted that it was something that worked for her while she was going through her depression. Going around and talking to some of the people I knew helped to raise my awareness on how many people are going through, or had actually struggled through depression, at some point. I was shocked by how many people I knew that went through or were going through the same fight I was battling. Coming to the realization that not only did I know people with depression, but those who I lived with and saw every day, who either fought or were still fighting it helped me gain motivation to seek help and take the depression on, head on. I believe that one of the main problems with depression is that people who suffer from it often feel like it is rare, and that they are the only one in their circle fighting it. When you feel like you're the only one who's going through something, it makes it a lot harder to get better because you don't want to risk telling people and having them look at you differently. If people were aware of not just how many people in the world, but how many people they know have, or have had depression, I'm positive you'd see tons more people seeking help.

I went to my first therapy appointment nervously and a bit skeptically, but with a completely open mind. I wasn't sure at all how it was going to go, but I was desperate, and ready to start feeling better so I tried not to worry myself about the details. Seeing that I wasn't sure what was going to happen, and I wasn't necessarily sure how I was going to react to the therapy, I thought it was a good idea to have my mom with me for at least my first visit. I imagined that she would do most of the talking while I sat back and listened to what Michelle had to say. My mom knew me and she was aware of how I felt at my lowest points so I thought I was fitting that she was present just in case I went numb and didn't want to talk.

Talking to strangers has always been awkward for me, and is weird for most people; talking to a stranger about your feelings is something most people can't even fathom, and for me was honestly a bit terrifying. Most of the time I couldn't even process my own thoughts or figure out what was wrong with me, how in the world was I supposed to express how I felt to a complete stranger. I knew nothing about this person besides her name, Michelle, along with the fact that my pediatrician knew her, had worked with her, and said that she was great (I mean what else was he supposed to say?).

When Michelle came out into the waiting room to get my mom and me, I started getting even more nervous. I knew at this point there was no turning back and it was time to face the music. I had been avoiding this for so long and built such a negative image of it in my head that it was a moment I was dreading for a long time, and it felt exactly as I had imagined – terrifying and anxiety provoking.

When we reached Michelle's office, she and mom began introductions and exchanged initial pleasantries. I was busy battling my own nervousness, sweaty palms, heart beating through my chest, and all kinds of thoughts and questions racing through my mind. I tried to do what my mom had suggested before, when struggling with anxiety, and breathe deeply while trying to quiet the negative voices in my head. I focused my attention on the introductory conversation and discovered that Michelle actually had a kind of calming spirit. It is said that developing a therapeutic relationship is like developing any other kind of relationship. There needs to be chemistry, shared vision, trust, and you actually should like and feel comfortable with your therapist. Almost immediately, I began to feel at ease in Michelle's presence. When it was my turn to talk, I was shocked at how easily I was able to express myself to her. I began to lay out how I was feeling, and the events that led up to my break down.

When I finally stopped, Michelle began to recap the things that I'd said, in. a reaffirming manner – validating my thoughts, and feelings in a way that made my struggles seem less shameful, and more normal than I'd ever considered. We got to work right away. Michelle began to methodically, explain what depression is, how it is an illness like any other illness, and how it develops and is treated. I began to understand how societal and cultural stigma had a great impact on my reluctance to seek help and to feel much better about taking the first step toward healing.

Leaving that first appointment, for the first time in a long time, I felt a sense of hope. For all those months, I was thinking so negatively that I was just waiting for something really bad to happen to me so this nightmare would be over. That's the only way I saw this thing ending, some tragedy that would put an end to my story. Going into that first appointment opened up numerous possibilities for me and I finally started seeing that light at the end of the tunnel. At first, I had been so against therapy for many different reasons, but I finally felt like it may be the first step to recovery for me.

Michelle had multiple ways of revealing to me what it was I was fighting and how to stop those things from affecting my everyday life. Some of the tools she used to educate me included charts and graphs, and things of that sort, which were very helpful to me because I consider myself a visual learner. Sitting down and looking at the charts allowed me to see, and therefore, better understand the origins of that negative thinking, along with ways to disrupt, and counter those thoughts. What I was beginning to discover, simultaneously was that I wasn't going through all of this alone. The various charts and diagrams she showed me had presented shocking statistics, leading me to realize that I really wasn't the only person fighting depression. It may seem like a silly way of thinking, but you can really get so down and confused that you feel like you're one of the few people if any in the world that are going through what you have to endure.

Being in that office and looking at all the depression materials and literature that has been printed, mass produced, and available for everyone, was shocking to me. I didn't know that there were so many people who suffered from depression and that there were actual solutions for it. When you have depression, most of the time you feel like you're drowning and there's no escape. My first therapy appointments completely opened my eyes to the other side. That other side was happiness and from that very first appointment, I was able to see happiness for the first time in a while. I knew it was going to be a tough battle, but this time I had found a weapon I could use effectively and that weapon was therapy.

As we continued our weekly sessions, I was able to take some of the things I learned in therapy and use them when I got home. A major challenge we attacked in therapy was how to stop my intrusive way of thinking. I wasn't sure when it started or where it came from but after working with Michelle, I realized that it stemmed from my depression in some way. It got to the point where it was almost impossible for me to think positively about anything at all.

No matter what the situation was, I would always look at the worst-case scenario. I was always worried about the worst possible outcome in every aspect of my life, and it started to make me worry about everything. When those negative thoughts came into my mind, I learned how to deflect them, by confronting the distortion of reality those thoughts often included, and to think about the positive side of things by reflecting upon the good things I had going for me, and counting my blessings. It's like being at therapy opened up another way of thinking for me and those intrusive thought weren't as strong as they usually were. The fact that I looked at them for what they were, and didn't look at them as reality helped to keep me in a better mood and prevented me from worrying about everything.

Michelle and I started talking about those thoughts and how to deal with them in the best way. The first strategy was maybe the most helpful of all for me. It was identifying the fact that you have intrusive thoughts in the first place. Then when those intrusive thoughts arise and you don't identify them as so, you start to feel like those thoughts are true. If you aren't able to recognize when your mind is playing tricks on you, and making it difficult to see the good in any situation, you may fall victim to those thoughts and start to allow them to take over your reality. Figuring out that I was having those thoughts and separating them from what was really going on what was a tactic that helped me tremendously. Even to this day, when I have a negative thought, I use some of the tools that Michelle taught me to use in order to calm myself down.

Another of those tools was to simply sit and think about the reality of a situation, and focus on what's really going on. Like I said, identifying that you're having these thoughts is important. You have to really dig down deep and think about what's bothering you. You have to start asking yourself a few questions like, "how realistic is it that this is really going on?" Often times like I said earlier, intrusive thoughts can allow you to look at the worst possible case in every scenario if you allow them to, so it's up to you to start questioning yourself. It's a fight that takes place mentally that's necessary for you to move on from that way of thinking.

One of the biggest parts of my life that was affected heavily by this way of thinking was my relationships. Relating to the people you love while battling depression is hard for numerous reasons. One of the main reasons is because when you're depressed, you often lose yourself in the mix of everything and it's hard to maintain a solid relationship with someone if you don't even know who you are deep down inside. The depression was causing me to act out in ways I wasn't used to and made me wonder what kind of person I was. I would often find very small things to get mad about in my relationship and use them for reasons to start arguments, with my girlfriend, Olivia and with others, including my mother. The impulsive thoughts I was suffering with caused me to look at the negative side of everything everyone did or said, and it caused me to sometimes lash out or shut down for no reason.

For the first time over the past few months, I felt like I was accomplishing something. I felt like I'd finally made some headway in this fight with my depression. I had new strategies, a new way of thinking and it helped me make it through each day. Often times, when one of those intrusive thoughts would come to mind and I would find a way to counter it, with thoughts that actually made sense, and that calmed me down a lot.

Chapter 8
Not Wanting to Live, but Not Ready to Die

"I didn't want to be alive…. I didn't want to see anyone else. I didn't want to see another day." – Michael Phelps, Olympic Gold Medalist

Before I began meeting with Michelle, the people around me continued to try to help me by offering their suggestions for help and treatment, I was stuck in my bubble, waiting for a miracle to happen. All this was happening while I started to get these horrifying thoughts that I never thought I'd have. I was starting to have this battle in my head over whether life was worth it or not. I thought the negative thoughts about being alone were bad; boy was I in for it. As the days went by, the thoughts got even worse. I started asking myself all sorts of scary questions like "why am I still alive" or "how would everyone feel if I was just gone". It scared the hell out of me but for some reason, I thought they would just go away. After days became weeks and I continued to fight with these thoughts of being done with life, those thoughts escalated.

They subsided, for a while when I first started therapy, but began to creep back in even after I began my work with Michelle. Despite the progress I made initially in therapy, I got to this point where I just didn't want to live anymore. I had enough of battling these crazy thoughts in my head and feeling like there was no light at the end of this miserable tunnel. I was especially down because I thought simply beginning therapy would cure me.

The interesting thing about how I was feeling was that the thoughts weren't necessarily suicidal. There was never a point where I really wanted to take my own life, but at that point, I really wished something bad would happen to me. I can't say what I wanted specifically, but I guess I can say I was waiting for something tragic to just happen to me so

I could reach the end of what was feeling like a never-ending nightmare. The ideas would get so intense that sometimes they scared me to the point where I felt the need to tell someone. This is something that a lot of people struggle with, and it makes the battle against depression way harder than it already is. When people get to a point so low that they don't want to live anymore, it's not the easiest thing to express to other people.

Letting someone know that you had lost your desire to live can be stressful for many reasons. One of those reasons is because it's hard to trust someone with that kind of information. Telling someone about what's going on in your head is a risk because you're trusting that person with something that you don't feel comfortable with most people knowing. The uncertainty of how someone will respond when you confide in them is enough to discourage you from letting them in on certain things. Something so serious as suicide or wanting your life to come to an end is something that may cause most people to go into panic mode. They want to help you but the assistance they're trying to provide may not be appropriate at the time or what you feel that you need. Some people may go to extremes like contacting your doctor or trying to get you to go to the emergency room for immediate help. Some of these may be good ideas, but at that time the most important thing you need is for someone to just listen. Luckily for me, my mom did a great job of being able to adjust to how I was feeling and did her best to help while not being too overwhelming for me.

I had found some hope after making the decision to seek help, and the work I was doing with Michelle was very helpful initially. I would do well during and right after the appointment, but in the days between meetings, I'd begin to "ruminate" again. I felt even worse, because I was disappointed by my perceived lack of sustained progress in treatment. For that very reason, I didn't want to tell Michelle about what I was going through and would skip appointments. My mom convinced me to finally talk to Dr. Siegel about the thoughts I was having.

Seeing that I'm very calculating and I always want to know exactly how things are going to go down to a tee, I had envisioned the conversation in my head prior to the appointment. I was thinking hard about how I would describe these feelings to my doctor. I didn't want to come off as someone who was on the verge of seriously hurting himself, or taking my own life because that's not where I was mentally. Honestly, I didn't know what to call what I was going through. I wanted to be dead but I didn't want to take my own life. It was a hard concept to process for me so I couldn't imagine having to explain it to Dr. Siegel. Wanting to die and being suicidal are two different things, but once you get in that doctor's office, separating the two isn't easy. I knew if I told him that I wanted to kill myself, he'd have to take some type of action that I wanted no part of. The last thing I wanted at that moment was to be stuck in a hospital room somewhere on suicide watch when I wasn't suicidal. I didn't feel like something that dramatic was necessary. I just wanted those crazy thoughts out of my head.

I did a good job of talking down the severity of my situation so I wouldn't have to stay at the hospital, but I was presented again with options that I didn't want to consider. Dr. Siegel revisited adding medicine to the therapy to help to make it more effective. He also suggested hospitalization, or a day treatment program – all of which were steps I was absolutely not interested in taking, especially the hospitalization or day treatment. As for the medication, I was already stubborn pre-diagnosis, so there was no way I was going to give in at that point. I left the hospital that day feeling even more defeated. I had engaged in therapy, thought it was working, only to crash again. At the time, there were two things that I didn't understand. One, that the road to recovery is seldom a straight path – that there are bumps, setbacks and relapses. Therapy often reveals things and open ups old wounds that take time and effort to heal. Two, that these are many instances where weekly therapy is not enough. At the time, I wasn't ready to hear those truths. I was just sinking again.

I knew something else was going to have to change. Even though I'd developed a great relationship with Michelle and adopted some strategies that worked when I was able to think straight and focus, I was still suffering in a major way. I still couldn't eliminate the anxiety or bout of deep depression. I couldn't bring myself to tell Michelle, and I didn't want to be locked away in a psych ward, so I wouldn't let Dr. Siegel know how bad it was. No one knew or seemed to understand how dangerous my depression was getting and I was running out of ways to verbally express it. I felt like I was doing a pretty good job of articulating how I was feeling to people, so it made it more frustrating when no one could seem to help me get better.

Chapter 9
Somebody Save Me

"Never give up on a person who has mental illness. When 'I' is replaced with 'We', illness becomes "wellness". – Shannon L. Alder

My depression was getting worse and I found myself looking for someone or something to blame for what I was going through. I didn't know what steps to take in order to feel better and I was waiting for someone to come take care of everything. What I was expecting was obviously unreasonable but when you're battling depression, most logic goes out the window. I was feeling like I needed to be rescued or saved in some way and I was running out of patience waiting for a miracle to happen. My mom was doing everything she could to help me, but I wasn't making it easy for her. She wanted me to take steps that I didn't feel like I was ready to take, and I started getting frustrated. At that time, I was still fixated on the silly idea that I would somehow just wake up one day and my depression would be gone. I started getting upset at the people around me and blamed them for my depression growing worse. It made it easier to process if I had someone to pin my depression on so I told myself most of the time that it was my mom and everyone else's fault. This made me bitter and I'm sure very hard to deal with.

Even though at the time I felt like I was drowning, there were many people around trying to throw me lifejackets, they just weren't the exact ones I needed. Honestly, I don't even think I can tell you what it would've taken to take me out of some of my worst depression episodes but my support system tried everything they could think of. The tried vacations, outings, gifts, new employment opportunities, and of course everyone tried to talk to me to help to convince me to help. They were constantly reaching out to make sure that I knew that I was loved.

While you're in the moment you don't think too much about it, but I'm sure I've received a few text messages and phone calls that actually saved my life. Nothing ground breaking, just simple messages, like "We are all here for you", "We are never going to give up on you", or just "We all love you and need you".

In the moment, I would normally ignore all the calls and messages because I didn't want to talk to anyone and I didn't think anyone was suited to help me, but some of what was said in the voice and text messages ultimately did end up saving me after all. Knowing that I had so many people who really cared about my well-being and wanted to see me doing better brought my spirits up a lot of the time, and brought me out of the rut I was in.

All that goes to show is that if you know anyone who suffers from depression and they also get into those funks where they don't want to talk to or be around anyone, it's never a good idea to give up and leave them alone. Just knowing that someone took the time to text or call you multiple times shows that they at least care somewhat, and that can make or break the whole situation. Sometimes it may seem redundant and like it's not working or you don't matter, but you do. When you text a friend or family member in crisis, and tell them you love them or you're there for them, you can ultimately save their lives. If I didn't have this support system, I don't know where I would be right now.

Chapter 10
Self-Medication

"I can't remember a day since I got out of college when I wasn't boozing, or had a spliff or something…(they are) pacifiers. And I'm running from feelings."
– Brad Pitt, highly acclaimed actor

If you allow it to, depression can be the first step to a series of unhealthy choices. If you don't get the right help, you may go looking for it in the wrong places. It's almost impossible to live with depression without finding some type of way to cope with those feelings you have to deal with. One of the most popular ways people cope with depression is self-medication of some sort. Before I was diagnosed with depression and it got to its worst point, I was a recreational marijuana smoker. It was something I'd do with a few friends a few times a week at college, mostly at night while we were just hanging out. Once I started getting more depressed, the feeling I got after smoking started to become one of the only times where I wasn't completely stressed. Smoking marijuana would help me to stop focusing on all the bad things that were going on and put them on the back burner for a while. It felt like a medicine that worked, at least temporarily, and I started becoming more dependent on it. I didn't think it was possible to be addicted to marijuana, and I wouldn't say I was even close to it, but I will say that for a while, it helped me do things that were difficult for me to do sober. Things that I struggled to do normally like eating and sleeping became easier for me once I smoked.

The way that you feel when you're under the influence of marijuana can really make you believe it's a cure for depression. I was having trouble eating but when I smoked, my appetite came back. It took me hours to sleep because I was either too anxious, or I was up thinking too hard about something, but smoking also solved the sleep issues. What I didn't realize was that I was slowly falling into this unhealthy cycle and becoming more and more dependent on having to smoke to feel comfortable. To me, it was a solution to the major, immediate issues I was having and I started looking at it as a healer. In the back of my head, I was aware that the marijuana wasn't going to cure my depression, but it was the only thing that was helping me cope with what I was going through.

I tried to keep my weed consumption to myself and a few close friends for as long as possible. After a while, I was tired of caring about what everyone had to say. I had opened myself up for everyone to see inside, by sharing my depression diagnosis, and I already felt exposed. Everyone felt like they knew what was best for me, and I'm sure none of their plans included the idea of smoking weed. Here I was again, dealing with something that carried a negative stigma. Hiding the fact that I was smoking so much became a task that I was just too tired to keep working at after a while. Once my mom figured it out, I didn't care about keeping it from anyone else, and it was somewhat a relief for me. Hiding it from her had been such a burden. My mom didn't completely freak out, probably because she suspected that I used to smoke occasionally in the past, but she knew it was different this time. She was concerned about how much I was using and what I was using it for, but her approach was all-wrong.

Often times when you're depressed, it can be extremely hard for people to reach you with what they say. It's a lot easier to just let everything go through one ear, out the other, and to continue doing what it was you were originally doing. My mom was so worried about my marijuana use, I'm not sure she was paying attention to her approach. She quickly lost my attention when she started immediately telling me all the negative things she knew about marijuana. Seeing that I was so defensive at the time, I was quick to deflect whatever it was she was saying and shut down immediately. When you're depressed, you crave for someone who genuinely understands what you're going through and once you notice someone doesn't really get it, you lose interest in talking to them. I was looking for solutions, and to just stop smoking cold turkey at the time wasn't going to be productive for me.

My mom is loving, protective and fiercely loyal, but also can be a very aggressive, straight to the point person, and that wasn't necessarily what I needed at the moment. She talked to me about family members that started out using marijuana and allowed it to lead them down the paths of more dangerous drugs and my use worried her. That information only added to my stress and forced me to do my own research. It's not like this was my first time anyway. I was a recreational smoker while I was in school and I was able to do perfectly fine in all my classes. Smoking never handicapped me before, and right now it was helping me. If I were going to stop smoking, it would be on my terms and because I thought it would be better for me. In my research, I found a lot of data that helped me make sense of why I was so comfortable using marijuana during my depression and why I felt like it was helping me. Soon I read that there were tons of other people who were suffering from depression and also using marijuana to cope, like Vietnam veterans, and others suffering from anxiety and trauma. The research I was doing reassured me that I wasn't harming myself by smoking. In fact, in the articles I was reading, smoking actually helped to alleviate symptoms of depression. Being as strong-minded as I am, all I needed to do was convince myself that the marijuana was a crutch I was using, temporarily, until I found a real solution to my problem.

Chapter 11
Self-Harm

"You have so much pain inside yourself that you try to hurt yourself on the outside because you want help." – Princess Diana of Wales

Within weeks of my first appointment, I completely crashed. Sometimes when I was severely depressed I got in the car and just drove. I didn't know where I was going, but for some reason driving had a way of calming me down. This particular morning, in between appointments, and during the time when I was avoiding Michelle, I woke up feeling really depressed, which at this point, was not unusual, but on this day, I didn't have the strength to fight it. The anxiety mixed in with the depression was overbearing for me and I was in a rush to get out of the house. Taking a drive seemed like the perfect way to relieve some of my stress. When I got in the car though, I felt differently than usual. My body got all-stiff and I got this urge to just sit in the car and not go anywhere. I was able to fight off that feeling, and motivated myself to start driving a little bit. All I did was drive down the street and around the corner before I started having an anxiety attack. I realized it wasn't safe to drive under those conditions so I pulled over on a side street a few blocks from my house.

For a while I just sat there with the car running, my mind was just racing with negative thoughts. I was in a downward spiral of depressing ideas and I felt like there was no escape. I had told people about this feeling before but no one was able to help me in the way I needed so I decided that I wanted to be alone. Wanting people to help you and know that you're struggling but also wanting to be alone is a fight I often battle in my mind. Here I was, sitting in the car, thinking about what I was going to do next. Those feelings of wanting to be dead were coming back and they were as strong as they'd ever been. For the first time in my life, I wanted to hurt myself.

At this point I started shaking, I was terrified at what I was going to do now that I've entered a mindset I've never been in before. I was feeling alone and hurt, and I wanted people to finally see how much I was hurting. I felt like I had done all I could to tell people what was on my mind and I started feeling like I didn't do a good enough job of explaining the severity of these thoughts. Of course, in therapy, I didn't tell Michelle how bad things were getting. For reasons that didn't matter at the time, I couldn't make myself.

The only thing I could think of that would finally show people what was going on was to physically harm myself. Again, I didn't want to kill myself, this was my "cry for help" moment. I used to sit and wonder why people cut themselves when I was younger, but now I knew. All those questions I had in my head for the people I saw in middle school and high school with cuts on their arms I could finally answer. That's because I had finally reached that point.

It's an unimaginable feeling that you could never understand unless you went through it. It's a feeling where you genuinely feel like you have absolutely no one in your corner anymore. After sitting there thinking for about thirty minutes I started looking around the car for sharp objects. While looking through my glove compartment, I found a box cutter. When I grabbed it, I just sat there staring at it for what felt like forever. At that point, my thoughts were getting even crazier. I started questioning myself about who I was and got even more depressed thinking about how far I had fallen. I had no idea what I was doing but I felt like at this point, this was the only option I had. After what felt like days of contemplation, I finally took the blade and put it to my skin. The closer I got, the more my hands started shaking uncontrollably. I started dealing with so many feelings and emotions that I got anxious and started profusely sweating. This isn't at all what I wanted, but I had made up my mind that this was somehow going to change things for the better.

Finally, I was able to gain enough courage to put the cold blade on my skin and started slowly scraping away. I was very tentative because this was the first time I ever even considered harming myself and I didn't want to cut too deep. I made the first cut but it was barely noticeable. I wanted people to know, I wanted it to be recognizable so then it may be easier for people to understand my pain. I now had one full cut on my wrist, but that wasn't the end. Now I had gone too far to look back, I convinced myself that I was slowly healing myself by letting out some of the pain I was dealing with. It started getting easier with each cut and I just kept going, One cut after the other. Slowly and precisely I would make cuts on my wrist lateral to each other, all the way down my right forearm until I got to my tattoo of my mother's name. This seemed like a good place to stop for me.

When I thought I was finally finished cutting, I sat back and looked at my wrist. I had about six cuts on the left side of my right wrist and about twelve cuts on the rights side. The cuts were all visible, some more than others, but I wasn't finished. I didn't feel like the cuts were a real reflection of how much pain I was suffering from on the inside and it wouldn't mean anything if it didn't completely stand out. I had a bunch of red scars on my wrist, but now I wanted to bleed. I was being consumed by this idea that the worse my wrist looked, the more people would understand how much I was suffering. No one seemed able to understand my pain through my words, so maybe they'll understand me this way.

I started going back over the cuts I had already made and went deeper inside them. I wouldn't stop until I started seeing myself bleed, then I was satisfied. It was like the blood was a symbol of all the pain I had and I was slowly letting it out. Not only that, but now I had proof of this pain, now people can't just listen to the words and judge how I'm feeling off of that, now they have a picture. When I was completely finished with the cutting, I took a minute to sit back and digest what had just happened. When I took a look at what I'd actually done to my wrist, I was shocked and terrified. I couldn't believe what I had done to myself. Ever since those days in middle school, I had told myself that this is a place I'd never get to.

At this point I had no idea what my next step was. Here I am sitting in my car with a box cutter in my hand, and one completely bloody wrist. My main reasons for doing it were because I wanted to release some of the pain, and let people know how much I was suffering. I didn't feel like I had released much pain at all from hurting myself, so now it was time for the cry for help portion to take effect. I'm sitting in the car wondering how I'm going to show the people closest to me what I had done and how low I'd gotten in my life. The first thing I thought to do was grab my phone and go to the camera. Part of me still was in disbelief and I started feeling like I was in this horrible nightmare. It felt like an out of body experience and I was living in some sort of video game. Nothing felt real anymore and I started taking pictures of my wrists.

I sat and looked at each picture for what felt like hours at a time. I zoomed into each one and got as close as possible to the cuts. Some of them were bigger and deeper than the others and I sat there numb for a while. What had I just done? More importantly, what was I going to do next? The first thing I did when I got super-depressed was contact my mom, so when I came up with the idea to send one of the pictures to someone, she was the first who came to mind. I wasn't thinking of how this could turn out at all, all I could think of was finally allowing someone to see the severity of my depression. I knew that it would completely shock her and everyone else around me because I even shocked myself. I would just sit there and look at those pictures for minutes at a time, and my wrist was starting to sting from all of the cutting I was doing. I didn't care, the last thing I was concerned about was physical pain, and at this point it seemed like nothing to me. At this point in time, I would've traded in my mental illness for any physical pain in the world. I sent a few of the pictures to my mom and waited for a response. I remember receiving literally dozens of panicking text messages from my mom trying to get in touch with me. What didn't occur to me was that she was out of town so she must've felt stuck, which is why she reached out to others in our support system for help.

I'd just started answering my mom's texts, telling her to leave me alone, when my phone instantly started receiving texts and phone calls from more and more of people – my best friends, brother and sisters, cousins, even my uncle. With my mom feeling like she was isolated from the situation, and that there was only so much she could control, she did what she felt like was the only option, contacting my closest friends and family members. At this moment, I started panicking myself. Things started spiraling out of control and I was conflicted on whether I should answer my phone or not. My mom and everyone else wanted to know where I was, but giving up my location was the last thing on my mind. The last thing I wanted at this moment was a bunch of people coming to where I was and making a huge scene.

I sent the pictures of my cuts to my mom because I felt like no one got it, and I hoped maybe this would be a wake-up call for her, and her alone – she was the one who always saved me, and couldn't this time. I didn't send them so that everyone I knew would know I was crashing and had started hurting myself. I was just looking for one person in the world who would finally understand the battle I was fighting, and the person I relied on most was my mom. The whole thing was starting to backfire on me and now I felt like I had run out of options. I ignored most of the calls and texts that I was getting, but a few people stood out to me and I felt like I had to say something. I didn't want to make people think I was trying to end my life and I really didn't want anyone to know what I was doing, with the exception a few people anyway, like my mom and maybe Olivia.

After about a half hour of people trying to figure out where I was, my older sister, Christian, pulls up in an Uber right next to my car. Now I'm dealing with all kinds of emotions including total shock, because I didn't know how the hell she found me, along with confusion, because I had no clue she was even in town! My sister lives in Washington DC. It's rare that I see her much anymore, so let's just say I was caught completely by surprise when she showed up. We've always been so close. She's only three and a half years older, but has been like a second mother to me. Since she went away to college, and stayed in DC after graduation, we haven't been in touch as often, but I know how much she loves and cares about me. Seeing her there, in that moment was a shock that I wasn't prepared for.

With the flood of emotions running through my head, and being embarrassed by what I had just done, I got out of the car and started walking down the street. I didn't want anyone to see me like that, let alone my big sister, who was a perfect angel to everyone, and who I admired and looked up to, so my immediate thought was to get far away from the situation. I started picking up my pace a little bit because I knew she would try to follow, and that some people were going to be looking for me knowing I was in the area. A few blocks from where I was parked, I ran into my big cousin Ron, who lives in the neighborhood and heard what was happening. At first, I was thinking of running past him but something told me to stop and listen to what he had to say. He's someone I was so close to, growing up, so I knew he had my best interest at heart.

After talking to him for a minute or so, he convinced me to stop running, to give him the box cutter, and to allow an ambulance to come and take me to the hospital. He just kept telling me to stop fighting everyone and to let them take care of me. Deep down, I was tired of running anyway.

I didn't know what to do next, so I was going to let someone else determine that. My sister arrived on the scene, along with my aunt, and uncle. By the time the ambulance arrived, I was strangely happy to see it. I was mentally and physically exhausted from the whole ordeal and now that people had a different idea of what I was going through, maybe it was time for me to start really healing. The EMT's checked my pockets and the rest of my clothes to make sure I didn't still have the blade on me so I could no longer harm myself and then they escorted me into the ambulance onto a stretcher. This was the most awkward, uncomfortable ride I'd ever been on. My sister insisted on riding in the ambulance with me to the hospital so I would feel a little bit more comfortable. Traffic at the time was crazy, so even with the emergency sirens, it felt like it took weeks to get to the hospital. While sitting there on the stretcher, arms and legs all buckled up, I was being bombarded with questions from the EMT's. They asked things like if it was the first time I've ever hurt myself or if I still had plans to hurt myself or hurt anyone around me. Even though it seemed like the conversation was nonstop and the questions kept coming, I couldn't do much but sit there, still. This numb feeling had consumed me to the point where all I could do was nod and shake my head at the time.

Throughout most of my journey with depression, I've done a pretty good job of communicating to people how I felt, but at this point, I had nothing to say. I was dealing with many different feelings, which varied from embarrassment to confusion. I wasn't concerned with what was being asked anymore, now I wanted to know what was going to happen to me. All the different possibilities of places I would have to go to because of the cutting and how everyone was going to handle it drove me crazy. Even though I knew I was sick, I didn't want to be hospitalized. I was afraid of what might happen to me if I was admitted to the hospital for a mental illness. Laying there in the back of that ambulance that day, I was terrified of where my life would possibly go next. Even though I was partially relieved, I felt worried that what happened to me next would be taken out of my hands and the thought of that terrorized me during that whole ride. I knew there were certain precautions that the hospital would have to take when I got there, due to the circumstances, but I was hoping I would be able to be part of the decision-making, in terms of next steps.

Before this moment, the whole time I'd been struggling with depression, I'd been in control of the progress, or lack thereof, that I was making and I didn't want that to change. As the ride continued, I started to scare myself more and more with these different possibilities flying around in my head. All this time, nothing could be done to or for me without my say so, but now; I knew that the next steps might be totally out of my control.

When we finally arrived at the hospital, the nerves started to get worse. Having my sister there with me proved to be a positive, seeing that this visit to the emergency room would be different than all the other ones I've been through. We'd agreed in advance, that she wouldn't force me to be admitted as long as I agreed to get help and share everything with Michelle. When I got pushed into the room, the reality of the situation started kicking in. I got dressed in the gown, and sat there on the hospital bed waiting to see the first doctor. All I could do now was sit there and contemplate. I was cold and felt so vulnerable and nervous.

Every minute or two I looked down at my right arm in disbelief. I still couldn't believe that I had actually done something that seemed so farfetched to me before. I would start thinking about what I had just done and then get distracted by the stinging those cuts were causing on my wrists and get lost. I would stare at those cuts for minutes, even though it felt like hours, and get consumed by what I'd just done. It caused me to start questioning myself and who I was, and that became a new mental battle I had to fight. I kept thinking to myself a phrase that some people around me were using that upset me. I would look at what I did and think, "The old Tim would never do that". The real question through all of this was, "Who is the real Tim?"

Depression can bring out a monster in you that causes you to take a deep look into the mirror and start to question what you see. All my life I had a certain perception on cutting and self-harm, and believed strongly and with certainty that I would never do it. Now here I was, sitting in a hospital emergency room with blood all over my wrist because I decided that was the only choice I had left. Over the past few months, I had done and said things that I would've never imagined coming from me prior to the depression.

After sitting there in the bed for a while, I came to the conclusion that I was very close to losing myself and that I needed to find the right help. Michelle had been great, but weekly talk therapy was not enough. Especially when I couldn't bring myself to tell her that I was still hurting. Right then and there I made the decision to stop being so stubborn and start to make more of an effort toward getting better.

Considering what I had done to myself, it seemed like a real possibility that I'd have to stay in-patient somewhere overnight for a few days. For me, that was one of my worst fears. I had heard stories of people who had been cutting and they were forced to stay in the hospital under some sort of suicide watch until the doctors were convinced that they weren't going to harm themselves any further. That's not what I thought I needed at all. The last thing I wanted or needed at that point was to be locked in a room in a hospital or facility somewhere, without any of my belongings, restrained to a bed. I knew that I needed help and this time I was ready to let someone help me, but not that way.

I kept looking at my arm and getting afraid thinking about what might happen to me, and where I might have to go because of what I did. Next, I started thinking about what I was going to say to the doctors when they came in. I didn't want to be disingenuous, but I wasn't going to say anything that I thought would get me "sectioned" somewhere. When you are suffering from mental health issues and you go to the hospital for help, sometimes they "section" you. Being sectioned happens when the doctors evaluate how you're feeling and what you've been going through with your depression, and then they figure out a solution for your treatment that involves a period of observation. The more serious your depression is, the more likely it is for you to be admitted to a psych hospital for evaluation and treatment for days or weeks. All I could think of was being transported from Boston Medical Center to some mental health program somewhere and having to stay there against my will. I was trying to avoid going through something I knew would only make matters worse for me.

When the first doctor came in and started asking questions, I tried to cover up my wrist. Obviously, that didn't work and she asked to see my right arm. The first feeling I can remember having was embarrassment. The idea of having to show people what I did to myself and not being able to fully explain it was something I was ashamed of. To me, what I had just done was something completely out of character and I felt embarrassed having to show off the injuries and talk about what happened. The doctor continued to ask me the same types of questions I'd been asked in the ambulance, and some that I'd been asked heard over and over before in the recent therapy sessions with Michelle, appointments with Dr. Siegel and even by those in my support system. "What's wrong?", "Did anything precipitate this episode?", "Am I using any hard drugs?" In addition, she asked if it was the first time I'd ever done anything to hurt myself, if I still felt like hurting myself or if I wanted to hurt anyone else at the moment.

I was sitting there in the hospital bed going through what felt like déjà vu, as a parade of medical professionals came to see me. These same routine questions were starting to really aggravate me and made me want to shut down. I was tired of being asked the same questions, I felt like people were just going through the motions with me and not really trying to get to the root of the issue. It was like everyone was doing what they felt like they had to do and nothing more. I continued to answer the doctor's questions while also being conscience of what I was thinking about earlier. I wasn't suicidal and I didn't want anyone to misconstrue what was going on and assume that was the case. Although I tried hard to make sure everyone knew I didn't want to kill myself, I did want everyone to know how deeply depressed I was and that I was battling these thoughts of not wanting to live on a daily basis. Believe it or not, there's a strong difference between those circumstances.

When they asked if I had a plan to commit suicide I always said no, and that was absolutely my truth. I never sat down and thought about taking my own life, but I would sit and get so down that I no longer wanted to live. That's how I felt and I wanted people to understand it for what it was. In the back of my mind, all I could think of was getting out of there and going home and seeing some of my closest friends so I could try to unload some of this eventful day. At that moment, it occurred to me how important and helpful my loved ones really were. I was surrounded by "professionals" with years of training and experience, and all I could think about was being with my friends and family.

All the doctors and nurses were really nice; one of them even got me to eat (which was an almost impossible task at the time) so I was able to calm some of the anxiety I was fighting with. Even though the emergency room visit was a little bit calmer than I anticipated, the one negative that pretty much cancelled out all the good things was the long wait between each person that came in. I would say there was about a forty minute to an hour wait between seeing each nurse or doctor and it drove me crazy. I was feeling so anxious and nervous, particularly during those long waiting periods. Each minute felt like an hour!

After I finished talking to each person they would tell me that the next doctor would be in shortly to talk about the next steps for me and my sister and I would sit there waiting for about an hour each time. The wait would be so long that sometimes my sister got up and went to ask the doctors when they were going to come see me. It was nerve racking to the point where I just wanted to get out of there, whether I was feeling better or not. It drove me to give even more quick, vague answers whenever the doctors did come in and talk to me. After a few hours in the pediatric emergency room, I was told I would be transferred to adult so I could get the necessary help those in the adult mental health unit. The wait for the transport took at least forty-five minutes and that gave me just enough time to have another minor anxiety attack.

I was getting more and more nervous because I had convinced myself that I was going to be sectioned and have to stay somewhere I didn't want to be. I'd been told that the doctors would talk to Michelle, and I was convinced that she would advise against it, but I wasn't sure that they could reach her or that they would take her advice.

I asked my sister to help vouch for me when the doctors came around, but she wouldn't agree to do so until I assured her I would never do something like that again. She was worried about me but she also knew that being admitted against my will wasn't the best option for me. After promising to be more consistent with my therapy and to choose another option to step up my treatment, Christian agreed to ensure the doctors that she believed that I wouldn't harm myself if they let me go home with her. I felt a little more at ease at that point, but we were still waiting for transport.

All this time I was sitting there in the emergency room. No one had cleaned up the scars yet. For hours, I was sitting there having to look at what I had done to myself and deal with the embarrassment and regret head on. Finally, a little while before I was moved to the adult unit, one of the nurses came into the room and noticed that nobody had cleaned up the wounds yet. She quickly went to get the supplies and came back to take care of the cuts. When she was all done cleaning them, she wrapped my right wrist in tons of gauze to prevent infection. Now here I was sitting there with what kind of looks like a cast on my wrist. The first thing I was thinking about was how I was going to hide these scars now that I had to wear this to prevent infection. It was either expose the cuts for people to see and possibly have to deal with an infection, or walk around with a ton of gauze on my wrist and have to deal with everyone asking what happened and others already assuming. When you're depressed you stress out about almost anything, and this became a big stressor for me. I knew some people in my life were already aware of what had happened, but I wanted to be able to have some control of how and when to tell people my side of the story.

After getting all bandaged up by the nurse, I felt like I had a huge target on my arm. When the transport person finally arrived, my nervousness and anxiety immediately resurfaced. Those negative thoughts that seem almost inevitable and are impossible to stop, came back strong. I started to get this nauseous feeling in my stomach because I wasn't sure what was going to happen next. One of the main triggers for my depression is uncertainty. With having to deal with those crazy, uncontrollable thoughts, you want to make sure whatever it is that's going to happen is predictable. You don't want to be involved in anything that causes you discomfort, or be around anyone who you're not completely comfortable around.

Not being sure about what was going on and or what was going to happen next was enough to send me over the edge. On the outside, I usually did a good job of managing my actions and emotions so no one really knew how I was feeling. On the other hand, inside I was going through hell. The same was the case in the emergency room when I was being transported to the adult unit.

I started telling myself that I was going to be sectioned somewhere and have to stay for weeks. Yes, that was probably the most dramatic scenario that could have occurred but that's how your mind works when you're fighting depression. The panic got worse as I contemplated how long I was going to be away from my family and friends and what my everyday routine was going to look like when I was at this imaginary program. I hated myself for what I had done, I thought some sort of karma was coming back at me fast and I couldn't stop it. Finally, I arrived at the adult unit of the emergency room at Boston Medical. The room was cold and a lot less fun and entertaining than the pediatrics section (obviously). I was used to being in the emergency room because of the medical issues growing up, but of course, I was always in pediatrics. I was used to the people there, the silly cartoon paintings on the wall, and the comfortable environment that was presented. No matter what was going on with me at the time, I always managed to have a sense of safety and comfort in the Pediatrics ER.

Once I had been transported to the adult side of the emergency, I was immediately ripped from my comfort zone. The only thing keeping me somewhat level-headed was the fact that Christian stayed with me the whole time. If she wasn't there, I'm not sure I would've been able to handle these transitions, especially given the emotional rollercoaster I was on.

The wait for the first doctor wasn't too long in the adult ER and before I knew it I was talking to a doctor about the possibility of going home. She was very adamant about making sure I was mentally stable enough to go home without the risk of doing anything further harm to myself. The same questions were being rephrased and asked over and over to make sure I was fine. It felt like she was just waiting for me to say something relatively alarming so it would give the hospital a reason to ship me off somewhere.

It felt like I was being interrogated, and I kept growing more nervous as the conversation went on. After she was done asking me questions, she shifted her focus to my sister. She asked Christian for her opinion on whether or not I was okay to go home. My sister kept her part of the deal we had made earlier and told the doctor that she believed that if I were allowed to go home, I would be surrounded by people and who loved me, and I wouldn't think to harm myself.

After this intense ongoing discussion, the doctor told us she was going to go over the evaluation and let us know what she thought. All the nervousness and anxiety I was fighting earlier in pediatrics were absolutely nothing compared to what I was feeling while waiting on the doctor's final word. I went into total panic mode and Christian had to do her best to talk me down. I was convinced that the cuts were going to cause too much concern for the doctors and they were going to choose to section me regardless of what my sister and I had to say.

A few minutes later, the doctor came back to share with us her opinion on what my next steps should be. She said that she agreed with us that I wasn't suicidal and it wasn't necessary for me to have to stay somewhere overnight for my depression. She did suggest that I go to a day program that would help me get on the path to recovery. I was shocked and relieved to hear that I could finally go home after this nightmare of a day. The whole process of getting my clothes and my phone back felt surreal at the moment. All day I had imagined being escorted out of the hospital into another ambulance, being taken to some facility somewhere, but here I was walking out on my own power. Now that the worry about whether I'd be released from the hospital was over with, it was time to figure out what steps I was going to take, in addition to seeing Michelle, toward beating this illness.

While we were leaving the hospital, Christian gave me a long talk about what we agreed to earlier in the ER. She wanted to make sure that I was sincere when I said I wasn't going to harm myself and if things ever got that bad that I would let her know. In the back of my mind, it was something I knew I would have to do if it came down to it. At that moment, she reminded me of my mom, and in her care, I felt protected. It had been an awful day, but I was grateful that she showed up when she did. Christian and I have always been close, but this ordeal brought us even closer. She'd been away at school for most of my high school years and stayed in DC after she graduated. I didn't realize how much I missed her calm, but firm spirit, and most of all, her love.

I was tired of being depressed and this time I was ready to do something more about it. Yes, I'd made the huge leap of faith and began therapy, but I had to face the fact that it was not enough, and I needed to be honest about the fact that I needed more help.

Chapter 12
The Backpack and the Bricks

Jay Z, music mogul, rap artist, on therapy: *"I grew so much from the experience. But I think the most important thing I got is that everything is connected. Every emotion is connected and it comes from somewhere. And just being aware of it."*

After the initial introductory session, Michelle asked me to list all of the things in my life that were stressing me out. At first, it seemed like an overwhelming task to do until she broke it down a different way for me. She told me to imagine that my life was like a backpack and all the stressors were items making it heavier. She asked me what the items in my backpack were and it became easier for me to separate my problems. For so long I had gotten so used to being sad that I had forgotten what was causing the sadness in the first place. The appointment that I had imagined was completely different than what was transpiring. I thought my mom would be doing all the talking but instead, she sat back and observed me start to take some of these things out of this imaginary backpack. One after the other, I listed something that was hampering me and we went over each topic a little bit. We analyzed each issue and sorted them out based on a few different categories.

One of the categories we used to sort out my different issues was by the severity of the particular stressor. We wanted to figure out what the core issues were so that we could attack the most severe, first. Another category we created was one through which we sorted which of the stressors were easiest to fix. Some things that were depressing me, like having to grieve over lost loved ones, were harder than others to recover from. Those were the things we knew would need more work to come to terms with. Some other things that were causing me a great deal of stress were a little bit easier to solve, like financial issues, and some of my posttraumatic stress from various events that transpired over the years, like car accidents, and incidents of community violence. Situations after which I probably could've benefitted from talking to someone, but never did.

For the first time in months, I was starting to clear my mind and I could feel my anxiety going down in that moment. All at once, I was letting everything out, I was putting it all out there for her to receive. It was weird, but it was working. There was never a feeling of discomfort while I was there, I felt comfortable exposing all of this information to someone who I felt really understood me. Another reassuring feeling about therapy is that everything you say during your session is 100% confidential. Knowing that I could say anything I wanted about anything that was going on in my life and it wouldn't get back to anybody allowed me to genuinely open up to my therapist without holding back. Even with someone you really trust, it's hard to share your deepest feelings because it seems that everyone has someone they tell everything to, so I worried that if I confided in someone, they may share my secrets with their one confidante. Knowing that nothing I said would get out, I let out literally everything. I went into deep thought about all the things in my life that were bringing me down at different times, and I let them out for my mom and my therapist to take in. I had so many things on my mind that it felt impossible to sort them out when I was alone, but now at therapy, sorting those things out was much easier. Not only was I sharing things out loud that allowed my mom and Michelle to understand me better, but I started understanding myself better.

Being twenty-one is already stressful as it is, add in depression and we have a problem. The natural stresses of finally entering adulthood are enough to cause depression on its own. Being in college, finally living by yourself can bring the realities of life to your attention faster than you may realize. The time between eighteen to twenty-two years old can be the most fun and the most stressful period of your life for many different reasons. For some, they have to deal with the pressure of school. Having to maintain solid grades in college because everyone is depending on you can be very anxiety provoking by itself. Add the fact that in some cases a child may be the first person in their family who went to college so they feel as though they have to do exceptionally well in order to make everyone proud. Another stressful part about being in school is the "What am I going to do with my life?" factor that we all deal with.

Even if you're in college and you have a major, there's a good chance that at some point you've sat down and thought deeply about what your next steps will be after you graduate. Where will I live? Who will I live with? What will I do for work? These are just a few questions you lose sleep over every night, trying to map out your life while figuring out how to maintain good enough grades to keep yourself and your family happy. All that mixed in with trying to figure out who the hell you even are and maintaining a social life at the same time can be too much to handle. If being in school was so stressful, you'd think not being there would make you happier, right? Wrong! There's a chance that not being at school during this time is even more stressful than being on campus somewhere. When I came home from school to seek help for my depression, I thought I would be allowed to take some time off and just relax. Little did I know, I'd have to answer questions everywhere I went that had to do with why I wasn't I school and do so without exposing all of my latest complications. When I did tell a few people the real reason why I came home, I was faced with even tougher questions that I was working really hard to avoid answering.

One of those questions was by far the biggest one and hardest to answer, "what are you depressed about?" I believe that at least one of the issues with depression is that nobody really understands the severity of it. Seeing that we're never really taught about depression, we develop a lot of unhealthy misconceptions about the illness. One of those misconceptions is that everybody goes through depression. A lot of times if you hang around a good number of people, sooner or later you'll hear someone say, "I'm depressed." Most of the time it comes after they miss the bus, or fail a test, or run out of their favorite food at home. The issue is, that none of those people are really depressed. If they are, it's not because of those small mishaps. People go around saying they're depressed all the time when they're not, and that does nothing but desensitize the word and make people take the illness less seriously. The lack of knowledge we have about depression adds to people having misconceptions about it and not taking it as seriously as they should. If we have everybody walking around thinking that they're depressed and saying so, we're not going to be able to focus on the ones with the real illness and help them get over it.

People continuously asked me "why" I was depressed, which was troubling, because sometimes I had no idea. When someone is depressed often you find yourself just sitting and just feeling defeated, for no particular reason. Sometimes you wake up and can't get out of bed, either you simply don't want to or sometimes, you feel like you just can't. You have no energy and no motivation and you couldn't explain why if your life depended on it. That's depression. For those who suffer from it, it's not always easy to put the feelings or the illness that causes it into words. Putting those horrifying thoughts and feelings you have, for what feels like no reason, into words can be hard most of the time. All those questions caused me to start questioning myself even more, but now about my illness.

Those questions caused me to look in the mirror and ask myself over and over what was actually wrong with me. At the time, I didn't realize that depression could be caused by a chemical imbalance and not simply by a series of tragic events. That makes it extremely hard to articulate in simple terms, why you're depressed. With so many people walking around saying they're depressed and still moving forward, why couldn't I? At the time, I couldn't find the strength to tell myself that those people weren't depressed and that's why they looked so strong on the outside, despite complaining about depression.

For a while, I questioned the severity of the depression and wondered if I was falling just because I was weaker than the average person. Being at home started making me feel even more lost without an identity. At least while I was at school I felt productive like I was where I was supposed to be, doing what I was supposed to be doing. I felt like I was on the right path even though I didn't specifically know where that path was leading. Now I was lost, and I had to repeatedly explain myself and feel a sense of disappointment and curiosity from each person I talked to. When I was in that room with Michelle, expressing myself, I was really starting to dig in and find the roots to this depression. That first appointment we laid everything out on the table. It's like we created an action plan for what we were going to do and how we were going to do it. I'm a person who loves to know exactly what's going to happen step for step so creating this map of solutions was great for me.

As we separated my personal problems into categories, the category that had the most difficult issues to resolve, included grief over the loved ones I'd lost along the way. One major loss for me is the loss of my grandfather. With my father being in and out of my life since I was young, my grandfather was the most important male figure in my life. He was my role model and someone I either saw in person or talked to on the phone every day no matter what. I never needed for anything as long as he was around and he made sure that literally everyone in the family was doing well, at all times. He was the patriarch of my family and my father figure so when he unexpectedly passed away, I lost myself. Not a day goes by where I don't think about my grandfather, so often times I allow myself to shut down about it. Like most people I'm sure, I've never been the best at grieving. Losing people is an occurrence that I've had to deal with way too often, but still can't wrap my head around. Losing someone who had such a huge impact on my life so suddenly was too much for me to fathom and to this day it tears me apart from the inside out. Being in my old neighborhood and seeing the house that I grew up in with my grandparents always present always gets to me. My grandmother, now suffering from Alzheimer's and dementia, now lives in an Alzheimer's facility, and after seeing her in the condition she's in, it's a battle for me to continue to go see her.

Chapter 13
Brick 1: Loss of the First Love of My Life – Basketball

"What is love? Love is playing every game like it's your last!" – Michael Jordan

Being born on the same day as Michael Jordan may have also added a little bit of fuel to that fire I had for the game. Ever since I could walk I was crazy about playing basketball. There are tons of pictures of me as a toddler, holding, bouncing, and shooting basketballs. I began watching basketball games with my grandpa and my mom, before I even knew how to walk. I had the "grow to pro" kiddie hoops, from a year old, and started playing organized ball at five years old. From that point, I knew what I wanted to do with my life. Ever since then, I would make sure a day wouldn't go by where I didn't play at least a little bit. My mom and grandfather had a regulation sized hoop installed in our backyard, so that I could play every day and I did. It didn't matter if I had others to play with or not - rain, snow, sleet or hail, I would shoot at least 100 shots daily.

My whole life started revolving around the game. I consumed NBA games, and studied playbooks, I played in multiple leagues at a time, went to basketball camps, all year round to make sure I was at the top of my game. I played in many neighborhood leagues as well as with my middle school team and AAU basketball travel team.
After dedicating my life to the game that I love, I felt like all at once my dream was snatched away from me. I got extremely sick at the age of 13 during the summer before eighth grade and ended up in the hospital ICU, needing a major surgery on my stomach. I had something called *"Mal-rotation with volvulous"* and it was described to me as a condition where many of my digestive organs were fused into a ball, with my intestines wrapped tightly around them.

It had been a birth defect that had never been detected or diagnosed. As I grew, the condition became more complicated and life-threatening. I had emergency corrective surgery in August 2010 and from then on, my basketball career was derailed. The surgery to eliminate the mal-rotation took place in August, but I was in the hospital for the better part of four months due to complications occurring through November of that year. The mental and physical battle of that illness and recovery took a toll on me, and I struggled to get back to myself. I can't begin to describe how down I was during that period of my life. Family, friends and my medical team did what they could to try to keep my spirits up, but between the physical and emotional pain, it was virtually impossible. Therapists and counselors visited me in the pediatric inpatient unit, but I refused to open up.

There were many "close calls" during that time, some of which involved me almost losing my life. There were severe infections, scar tissue blockage, severe nausea and vomiting, and serious medication errors, just to name a few. For a while, after the hospitalizations were finally over, I was just happy to be alive. It was really hard to get back to who I was on and off of the court after the illness. Physically and emotionally I was a completely different person and I felt like my hoop dreams were slowly fading away. Being away from the game for so long was devastating for me in so many ways. One of the most important aspects of my game that was lost along the way was my confidence.

Being down in the hospital for so long not only took away my strength physically, but I became a lot weaker emotionally as well. I pretty much lost my identity on the court and felt like I had to find a new one and become someone different now that I've overcome something so devastating. It seemed like the old me wouldn't cut it and I started trying to re-create my basketball game and myself. That loss of confidence didn't stop me from returning to middle school that year and being a part of our basketball team's undefeated championship season but it carried all the way through high school, where it led to my decision that I was done playing ball. I simply didn't feel like I could excel the way I had before. If I couldn't be the best, I didn't want to play, at all. This was one of the hardest decisions I ever had to make, and something I still think about to this day.

Up until that point, I was used to being identified as a basketball player everywhere I went. For some reason, people could just look at me and guess that I was a ball player, and it would make me feel good to know that other people saw in me what I saw in myself. Going through high school and not playing ball was tough for many reasons. One of the toughest was the fact that some of my closest friends were playing ball. They kept trying every year to convince me to play, but I refused. Saying "no" to them was hard, but watching them play was even harder. I wanted to be out there with them so badly but deep down I knew I wasn't up for it. My confidence was shot. That was a struggle I wouldn't wish upon any other athlete no matter what.

I was so used to just telling people I played basketball and them being so caught up in that, they didn't bother to ask me about anything else. I never had to sit and think about who I was outside of basketball, but after my illness, while I was in high school, which is a stressful time under any circumstances, I had to find myself a new identity. No longer would I be known as the kid who can ball, but now I had to make a name for myself in another way. I didn't think about it back then, but looking at it now, that was one of the biggest loves of my life and I lost it before I was ready. Now I realize that struggling through that painful time in my life was traumatic. It forced me to find myself

75

all over again, and although I didn't know it at the time, I was sinking into a deep depression.

In fact, I now strongly believe that not playing basketball anymore was the first major "brick" in the build-up to my diagnosis of major depressive disorder. I was able to continue to cope, but the illness, recovery, and end of my hoop dreams was devastating.

Chapter 14
Brick 2: Biba's Illness

"A grandma is warm hugs and sweet memories. She remembers all of our accomplishments and forgets all of your mistakes." – Barbara Cage

My grandmother, Dolores Craft, known to us as "Biba", was a force to be reckoned with – strong, smart, quick-witted, and always stylish, classy, and a community leader. She had grown up in Boston, and it seemed as if everyone knew and respected her. Biba worked for a community-based, educational organization for over 30 years, and was committed, along with my grandfather, to raising a family built on a foundation of pride, respect, and commitment to each other and our community. She was tough in many ways, but had a very tender place in her heart for her grandchildren. I was the youngest in my generation of the family, and with my medical challenges, spent a lot of time in her care, especially after her retirement. I didn't begin school until kindergarten, and she and my auntie Charlotte took care of me. My mom would complain that I was being spoiled rotten, but I learned much about family, the world and myself from those early days with my Biba.

Ever since I started going to school in Brookline, I had gotten used to basically the same routine every day. I would either get dropped off at school or get on the school bus in the morning. In the afternoon after school, I would always take the school bus straight to my grandparents' house. That was my routine, my cycle, and I wasn't expecting it to ever change. I was used to coming home to seeing both of my grandparents every day, and most of the time they had something, delicious already waiting for me to eat when I got there. Both of them were great cooks so I was more than pleased when either one of them stepped into the kitchen. My mom joked that we ate four meals per day, because my grandparents would cook a full meal and have it waiting for their grandkids when we all arrived from school.

If I was sick and had to stay home from school, or when my mom was at graduate school in the evenings or away on business, that's where I would stay. My grandparents' house was my safe haven, not just for all of our family, but for years it had been a safe haven for others in the housing project too. Both of them did everything to make it feel that way. My grandfather did a lot of running around so he wasn't always home, but my grandmother was almost always there. We sat around and watch our favorite shows every day, and ran errands together a lot of the times. She would cook me whatever I wanted, whenever I wanted it, and when I was sick, she made sure that I was more than well taken care of. My grandmother and I shared a special bond, and completely adored each other. She was warm, fun, funny, loving, nurturing and protective. Biba was always my soft place to land and I made sure that she knew how much I loved and cherished her.

Around the time of my sophomore year of high school things started changing with my Biba. She started asking me the same questions over and over again, and had a hard time remembering even the most basic things. My mom and the rest of my family noticed a slight change as well, but we weren't sure what was happening. It felt like she had changed in the blink of an eye, and she went from being one of the sharpest people I knew to not being able to work a telephone or microwave. Her memory was fading fast, and it was both shocking and scary. She and my grandfather were the best cooks I knew, and before I knew it, our routine changed from her cooking me all kinds of meals one day, to me having to warm up microwave dinners for her the next. I didn't understand it, and I felt like I was slowly losing her.

She was so independent before, she took the bus or got everywhere she needed to go with no assistance. Now she had to depend on everyone else around her to perform even the most basic tasks, like make a phone call or get dressed. I used to be able to go to my grandmother for anything from advice to homework help, if I was hungry, or needed anything at all, and now I had to help her learn how to change the channel on the remote, over and over again. It was all happening so fast nobody really knew what to do about it. After multiple trips to see her doctor, she was diagnosed with both Alzheimer's disease, and dementia.

Once I found out what my grandmother was suffering from, I started doing my own research. I looked up what Alzheimer's and dementia were, and tried to find the cure for them. When I found out there was no real cure for either one of the diseases, I was distraught. My grandmother, my Biba, one of my best friends in the world was declining mentally and suffering, and there was nothing I could do but be there for her.

It was extremely hard watching her make that slide and fall deeper into the illnesses, but I did everything I could to make sure she was still comfortable and happy. The dynamic in my life had changed so fast that I had no time to really think about it or digest it. Instead of coming home to her warm greeting and hot meal, I had to make sure grandma ate, that she was safe, and she was doing okay each day. We all pitched in and created a sort of schedule, but the afternoons and much of the weekends were my responsibility. I often spent the night on Fridays and Saturdays to help Grandpa who had his own health challenges, to keep her comfortable and safe. Mom went by in the morning and again at lunchtime. My older cousin Darren, and Keya and Darius helped out too, but Christian was away at college.

It started getting worse and she started struggling to remember people's names. I understood that it was a normal stage in the progression of the diseases, but when she would look at me and not remember who I was, it would crush me. She wasn't gone but I felt like it was time to start grieving the grandmother I used to have. It felt so wrong for me to do, but she was such a shell of herself at that point that it was hard for me to look at her and see the same person. The grief and the guilt, at times, was almost too much to bear.

After a few months past and we realized that it was too much to keep her at home and try to make sure she was safe at all times, we were forced to move her to an Alzheimer's facility where she would be well taken care of. It was a decision that nobody in my family loved, but at the end of the day, it proved to be the best option for her. Everyone had to put their own selfish ideas behind them and worry about what was the best situation for her. She would get up at home and randomly walk around outside, at random times of the night and day and it just wasn't safe for her anymore.

Now after school, I had to get used to going to the facility to see my grandmother, instead of going to her house, and being able to unwind. My life had been flipped upside down and it was a change that I was nowhere near ready for. Thinking about my grandmother and the state she was in would eat at me all day every day and it all was feeling like a sick dream to me. I couldn't wrap my head around what was happening and it was so random and blind-siding that it completely floored me and took me out of myself for a while. My life was feeling so incomplete without that special bond I shared with Biba. Going to my grandparent's house and having everybody there was such a big part of my life that had been taken so quickly and unexpectedly that I was left feeling alone and empty for a while. Even though she was still around physically, I felt like I had lost my grandmother for good, and that became a cloud that hung over my head everyday thereafter. Again, a major "brick" in the proverbial depression backpack.

Chapter 15
Brick 3: Losing Poppy

"People who have previously struggled with acknowledged or unacknowledged depression, the death of a significant other can be the catalyst that brings the depression to the foreground."
– Dr. Michael Miller, Editor of the Harvard Mental Health Letter, Psychology Today, "When does grief become depression?" March 21, 2012.

My grandfather, Poppy, was my everything. There hasn't been a point in time where I consistently had my father in my life and my grandfather was the one to fill that gap for me. William James Craft, Sr. was the strongest, bravest, most intelligent man I knew. He was a former Marine, having enlisted as a teenager after the death of his father, right around the time that the military became racially integrated. Despite his struggles with racism, and classism throughout his life, he was clever, resilient, and determined to make a way for his family. He and Biba were married for 49 years, when he suddenly passed away, and it shattered our family's sense of security.

There wasn't a day that went by when I didn't at least talk to my grandfather. Pop was the heartbeat of our family. He was no nonsense with an almost God-like commitment to honor, justice, and integrity, qualities that we all inherited from him. He was so wise, patient and even tempered with all of us, but if you threatened his family or threatened the sense of balance and unity he created within our family, you had a fierce force to contend with. Everyone in our family and community felt that they had a special relationship with him. Pop made everyone feel that way. He was the patriarch of our family and neighborhood and took that role very seriously. He was big and strong, yet had a laugh and smile that would warm the world. He taught me everything I needed to know about being a man, and in the most loving way.

He did everything for me and was that person I knew I could always go to no matter what the situation was. He always saw the best in me and everyone else, and that ability was what allowed him to be such a giving person. Since my dad at best would be in and out of my life (mostly not in it at all), my grandfather made sure I never went without anything and did any and everything for my mom and my siblings as well. Once in a while I would still get caught up in the fact that my dad wasn't around and it would get me down, but my grandfather was such a strong father-figure that he filled up most of that void for me.

He was by far the rock of my family and he was great at making sure nobody ever needed anything. He helped increase my love for basketball and the Boston Celtics by taking me to tons of Celtics games every year. We would go to the games, talk on the phone about them, or watch them together. I'm a huge sports guy now, and that's all thanks to my grandfather bombarding me with Patriots, Red Sox, and Celtics games ever since I can remember. He's the most generous person I've ever met and would put anyone he cared about before himself everyday he lived. When I was in middle school, the bus dropped me off at my grandparents' house every day after school. His neighborhood is where I met a lot of the friends I still have today. I built many strong relationships there, and my grandparents were such a huge part of my life.

When I found out that I lost my grandfather, I was destroyed. I felt like my whole world had stopped and come to an end all of a sudden. In that moment, my whole life had been changed and I was very well aware of that. I was filled up with so many emotions I didn't know what to do. I obviously felt like crying but it didn't seem real so the tears couldn't come out. It's like I had lost my best friend and my father all at one time. We talked so much that to this day I can still have a full conversation with him in my head and feel like we really had a sit down. I didn't know how I was going to continue on living without someone who was such an enormous part of my life. When I was in the hospital for months, my mom stayed with me every night and my grandfather came up there every night to see me no matter what the conditions were. I could hear his cane clicking on the ground from down the hallway, and I immediately got excited. My dad didn't come see me once while I was in the hospital from August to November, but my grandfather didn't miss a day. No matter what I was going through in my life, he was that person that made me feel like he could make it all better (as he always did). When he died, I was so shocked and broken that I did my best to put that in the back of my head and try to move forward as soon as possible. I knew that if I allowed myself to grieve, it was going to be a long, hard process, and I didn't think I was ready at the time. Little by little over the past few years, I have allowed myself to sit and get caught up in all the emotions that come with the death but these moments are rare. There is a still ton that I haven't let out yet, and I'm sure it slowly eats at me. The day he passed away, he took a large piece of me with him that I know I won't ever get back.

He and Biba led our family for five decades, with a dedication to ensuring that we all felt loved, safe and united. They made sure that we all set positive goals, expanded our horizons and reached our greatest potential. I can't overstate the sense of loss, fear of the future and just complete despair I felt. Yet another cripplingly heavy "brick" for me to try to carry.

Chapter 16
Brick 4: Relationship Troubles

"Dating me means dating my anxiety, and my random bouts of depression; It means dating my panic attacks at 11pm or 2am or 5am or anytime of the day for that matter; it means dating my mood swings where I get really upset over everything about me and all my insecurities, and how I'm not good enough because I'm never good enough." – Feggotdesu

Before the depression really kicked in, I was in a relationship for about four years with my girlfriend Olivia. We met freshman year in high school and started dating junior year on Valentine's Day. Our relationship took off and got serious immediately. We spent a lot of time together, our families got really close and our lives were intertwined in many ways. It hasn't been all easy though given that since high school, we had been battling different issues due to the normal high school drama (rumors, gossip, jealousy, etc.) but we always pulled through. This fight was different for us; she knew what I was going through so she tried for as long as she could to hold on. After a while, being in a relationship with someone fighting depression can definitely take a toll on you. First off, being with someone who doesn't love themselves, as people probably already know, can make for unhealthy habits in a relationship. I hated myself for a long time during my relationship, and it caused multiple issues along the way.

I was never a person who lacked confidence growing up to say the least, but all of a sudden, I couldn't even stand to look at myself. It began to make my insecure about myself and those insecurities cause various problems in my relationship. I started believing I wasn't good enough for anything or anyone so it was hard for me to come to terms with someone loving me so much.

When someone loves you more than you love yourself it can become very troublesome for your relationship. That's another battle I was fighting and after a few months of unnecessary arguments, many changes internally, and my bitterness and lack of motivation, we saw no other option but to split up for a while. As you could imagine, losing someone I'd had and grown so used to since high school was like having to grieve all over again. We had broken up so many times in the past months that I knew we'd be back, but it was the uncertainty of when that was killing me.

Just because my relationship had to go on the back burner for a while didn't mean those negative thoughts went away. I would find myself every day, worrying and stressing about my relationship even more now that the official title wasn't there. Even though she hadn't once given me a reason to believe she wasn't happy in our relationship and she is one of the most loyal people I know, believing the reality of the situation was hard for me. We were broken up, but she never went anywhere. She constantly texted my mom almost daily to check on me from a distance and make sure I was doing okay. Periodically she would even text me and we would talk and touch base for a little while before going back to the non-communication. All that was great, but it really made things worse when I started thinking about it. All it really did was make me want something back that I wasn't ready for, and that was my relationship. She had gotten tired of being like my verbal punching bag and neither of us were ready to take the other back just yet.

Those negative thoughts would tell me different reasons why we weren't together and they always included the idea that she didn't love me anymore. I would convince myself that she left because she couldn't take who I was anymore and that we would never get back together again. When you get deep into those negative thoughts, the reality of situation becomes irrelevant. In the back of my head, I always knew we'd end up back together, but the heaviest thoughts had to do with things that didn't really make sense to me. All the uncertainty about my relationship and what was going to happen next was enough to take up it's own category in my backpack of stressors.

Depression can change you in so many different ways; it can affect how you treat people and therefore, cause a strain in some of your relationships. Having the feeling that I was alone and that no one understood me led me to start saying and doing things that were completely out of character. For one, I was a lot more disagreeable and argumentative than I ever was before. The depression was causing me to see everything in a negative light and that led to me starting a lot of unnecessary arguments and rifts between myself and those who were close to me. I got into such a bad cycle of being mad over small things and picking senseless arguments, that it started to take a toll on my four-plus year relationship. Olivia was supportive but I understood that the person I was at the time was almost impossible to deal with on a day-to-day basis, so we took some time off to let me heal. However, she never really went anywhere, because she constantly kept in contact with my mom to see how I was doing and offer any support I needed.

Chapter 17
Brick 5: Dealing with Money Issues

"Being in debt, broke and unemployed can lead to depression, but the converse is also true: depression can precipitate financial meltdown." - Richard Zwolinski, & C.R. Zwoliski, Psychcentral.com

Most college students and kids who just finished high school have many of the same issues. One of those problems is maintaining a steady income. After high school, most people choose one of a few different paths to go down. If affordable, the most popular one is going to some college, another is finding a job and just working to try and save up some money, some do both, and some do neither. No matter what path you choose to follow, the majority of young adults after high school graduation start to worry about their future and how they're going to be able to take care of themselves. The pressure starts getting stronger as you get older and the people around you start expecting you to become more independent and self-sufficient. The pressure that you receive from the people you know mixed in with the natural pressure that you already put on yourself can be enough to cause some depression or add to it if you are already suffering from it. As independent as I am, I wanted to stay in school and work a job at the same time, like a lot of people I knew. As much as I wanted to take complete control of my life and start to take more responsibility, my depression came in and put a stop to all that positive thinking.

One of the most prevalent symptoms of depression is the loss of motivation that it gives you and that factor made it almost impossible for me to do what I planned to do. Not only did it eventually drive me out of school, but it also ripped away my motivation to find a job as well. All of a sudden, I was fighting myself in my head over and over, contradicting my own thoughts and ideas because the depression was winning the battle. I wanted to be in school because I felt like that's where I should've been. I wanted to work a job because I wanted to build something for myself, but I had zero motivation at all. My hardest battle for months for me was getting out of my bed. I would lay in bed every morning for about an hour and contemplate whether I was going to get up or not. Half the time I convinced myself that it was better for me to just stay in all day and sulk. I knew that I wouldn't be able to maintain a job under these circumstances and that made me even more depressed. Depression can cause you to go into an uncomfortable cycle of wanting to do things but not having the motivation or energy to fulfill them.

My mom gave me a job at the non-profit organization she founded called Smart from the Start, which is a child development and family support program in Boston. Working there allowed me to be as comfortable as I could while dealing with my depression. Most of the time while I was at work, I was driving around which was good for me. I would have to drive around the city and deliver books to some of the businesses my mom's program connected with and it allowed me to feel productive and positive as well. Seeing that my mom's program has been running for about ten years now, I know a lot of the staff and have known a few for a very long time so being at Smart makes me feel at home a lot of the time.

Working for my mom isn't without it's challenges. Some of those challenges includes working there during down times. Sometimes I don't have enough work to do, or I'm given work that is tedious or requires sitting in one spot for too long and when my depression and anxiety is at its worst, that drives me crazy. Idle time is something that can be horrible for you if you have depression because it creates space for those negative thoughts to arise and play around in your head since there is nothing distracting you. Being at work was a blessing and a curse for me during the height of my illness. Some days were easier than others, but at least I had a job. It made me feel like I had a sense of purpose in life at a time where finding that main purpose felt impossible.

Going to my appointments allowed me to somewhat open up again. The tasks that seemed so hard to accomplish weren't so taxing to me anymore. The struggle of getting out of bed became less severe and after a while I was able to maintain a job working for my mom and started setting goals for myself. Being proactive in the efforts to get better allowed me to revisit the goals I had set for myself before I got sick. All of a sudden, I could once again see myself accomplishing things that I had set out to accomplish before the severe depression set in. At one time, I didn't see a future for myself at all, but now there was a future I could see, and it is a bright one.

Chapter 18
Brick 6: Secondary Trauma

Secondary Trauma is defined by the National Child Traumatic Stress Network as follows: *"Secondary traumatic stress is the emotional duress that results, when an individual hears about the first hand traumatic experiences of another. It's symptoms mimic those of Post-traumatic Stress Disorder (PTSD)".*

Growing up in an environment where community violence is an everyday occurrence, and violence and discrimination against people who look like me is definitely stressful. I didn't realize the impact it can have on someone already struggling with depression.

I know people very close to me over the years who lost their lives to street violence, yet never anyone in my immediate family, so I shook my head and felt a sense of sadness and loss, but never really considered how it was affecting me. I began to feel differently about where I hung out, more cautious. Places where I'd grown up, like my grandparents' neighborhood, where all of my families and childhood friends lived, no longer felt like safe havens anymore. It began to feel kind of like my safety net was loosening and I was unsure if it was really safe anymore. That can be extremely detrimental, particularly during a time when I needed certainty and security in my life.

Watching or hearing the news reporting on the senseless murders of youth by the police or being stopped and harassed were so troubling that it became difficult to hear about the incidents any longer. It makes me wonder how young kids are affected and worry that their issues are probably not being properly acknowledged or addressed.

"Most children and adolescents with traumatic related psychological symptoms are not identified, and consequently do not receive any help. Even those who are identified as in need of help frequently do not obtain any services. This is especially true for children from ethnic and racial minority groups and for recent immigrants, who have less access to mental health services. Even when children are seen for mental health services, their trauma exposure may not be seen or addressed." Children and Trauma, 2008 Presidential Task Force on Posttraumatic Stress Disorder and Trauma in Children and Adolescents, American Psychological Association, apa.org

They teach kids about sex education, and bullying in school now, which are both important topics of discussion, but there is very little about depression or trauma, unless there is a mass shooting or suicide within the school community. Even under those circumstances, counselors come in for a while and then things go back to "normal".

With the increasing number of young children committing suicide, engaging in violent acts of their own, bullying others, or indulging in self-medication, it is past time for educators to begin to take seriously their responsibility to teach parents and children about trauma, depression and how to recognize it, and get real help. The stigma is still pervasive in society and that along a lack of knowledge is only hurting our kids.

Chapter 19:
The Medication Equation

"When you are clinically depressed the serotonin in your brain is out of balance. So, I take medication to get that proper balance back. I'll probably have to be on it the rest of my life." – Terry Bradshaw, NFL Hall of Fame Superstar.

As I started going back to therapy on a consistent basis, Michelle and my mom tried to slowly bring back the idea of another helper for my depression, taking meds. The cutting incident had me convinced that I was going to have to consider other options in addition to my sessions with Michelle. After seeing the results of the therapy and realizing that not only was there nothing wrong with it, but that it had actually begun to help me tremendously, I started giving medicine more serious consideration. I was still very hesitant about it because to me, there was a huge difference between starting therapy and taking medicine. For me the two were very different, but to my mom and Michelle, they were complementary, and together, would provide me better support as I worked to heal. My mom has her masters in counseling psychology so she was well aware of what I was going through and like Michelle, thought that the therapy with the meds was the best way to go. It would allow me to get what I needed in terms of talk therapy and getting things out, and also helping out the chemical imbalance caused by depression with the meds. Michelle started listing the different medications to me and honestly, they all kind of sounded the same.

To me, it was all medicine and I wanted no part of it. I listened to what Michelle was saying but in the back of my mind, I couldn't envision a scenario where I wanted to start taking any type of medication. They all sounded the same to me and the question for me was more if I was going to take anything at all rather than what it was I was going to take. Leaving my appointment that day, I knew I had a big decision to make. I knew that the therapy was working, but given the pain I continued to struggle with, it was only working to an extent. I knew, at that point, that I couldn't cure my depression just by attending my sessions with Michelle no matter how well they were working out for me in the beginning. Therapy did help with some things, but I was still having some major issues. The depression was still stronger than ever, and the negative thoughts still came. The tools I'd mastered in therapy were helping me cope in the moment, but not taking the depression away. It's like I was fighting the same battle as before, but now I just had one new weapon to fight with. It was clear that I needed another in my arsenal, and despite my concerns, medication was it.

I was starting to come around to the idea of maybe trying to take something. Even though there was that general stigma about taking medicine for mental health, mixed in with my own reservations, I had a feeling that this might be just what I needed to help push me even closer to recovery than the therapy alone. After a few weeks of talking to my mom and Michelle about adding the medicine to my fight against depression, I gave in and decided I would start taking a medicine called Prozac. At first, I was very nervous about starting the meds because I was always worried about the side effects. I'm sure there are millions of people around the world who have second thoughts about taking medication because they saw or heard all of the side effects the medicine can potentially cause.

One of the biggest side effects of Prozac is that it may cause increased thoughts of suicide. This is something that I'm sure scares the life out of everybody who considers taking medication for anything, especially depression. Having depression can bring on those suicidal thoughts by itself, so taking something that may make those thoughts even stronger is something that scares a lot of people away from taking anything at all. These are some of the things that pushed me away from the idea of taking meds but going to therapy helped shed some light on the fact that the side effects usually never actually happen and the probability of you experiencing any of them is really low. That gave me some reassurance and the confidence I needed to decide that medicine was my next step towards healing.

In order to start taking the medicine, I needed to book an appointment with another doctor, a psychiatrist. The psychiatrist is responsible for prescribing my medicine and keeping up with me to make sure I was doing okay, and not experiencing any setbacks or side effects.

The psychiatrist's name was Dr. Spencer and the conversation with her made me feel ten times better about taking the Prozac. The appointment was nothing like I expected, just like the therapy. I don't even think the purpose of the Dr. Spencer appointments is for therapeutic reasons, but they work as so. She knew more about the medications than anyone else I talked to about them, so I knew when she was talking that I could trust what she was saying. She was not only able to inform me about the different meds and their good and bad aspects, but also told me what she thought was the best for me, personally. She talked to me extensively about the side effects and made me feel more comfortable about not worrying about what would happen to me if I started taking Prozac. Aside from the medication discussion, the first meeting with Dr. Spencer was helpful for me in a few other ways.

Once again, I had to tell the entire story of my depression from the beginning, but just like in my first therapy session, it was a helpful experience. Going back and talking about when I first got depressed to the current day always helped me out. Just by sitting there and talking to someone about what I was going through and knowing that they understood me allowed me to feel a sense of relief because I was allowed to let out a lot of feelings and ideas that were bothering me. I felt comfortable talking to Dr. Spencer and in that first appointment, I let out everything. I knew the appointments with Dr. Spencer would only take place once a month when I needed a new prescription so I felt like I had less time to get out things than I did with Michelle. I felt pressed for time so I made sure to quickly but thoroughly go through all of the things that were adding to my depression.

Dr. Spencer was completely understanding when it came to everything I was going through and validated that it was okay to feel how I was feeling. Even though I know I've been through a lot, I often beat myself up about being depressed as if I could control it. Dr. Spencer listened to all that I told her I was going through and let me know that with all I'd been through, it made complete sense as to why I was suffering from depression. Both of us together explored my multiple traumatic experiences, which allowed us to understand how I got to where I was we agreed that it was time to move forward. This was huge for me because all this time I was looking for validation for my depression and I felt like I finally got that with Dr. Spencer. Seeing her reaction when I told her some of the things I'd been through assured me that it was okay to feel the way I was feeling as a result of all the hardships I'd been through and had been trying to get over. She looked to be in shock when I explained to her some of the things I'd experienced over the past few years. I noticed her reaction and it started to erase all of the ideas in my head that had to do with me being depressed for nothing.

Michelle and I had already laid out the different tragedies and hardships and how we were going to attack them, but telling Dr. Spencer all of these things for the first time and seeing her reaction allowed me to look in the mirror and be more understanding of the situation I was in. I stopped feeling like such an outcast and started looking at myself as being able to possibly move forward now that I was more self-aware. I felt like I was in that office for hours, peeling more and more layers off with each story I told. By the time the first session was over, I remember being genuinely happy because I felt like progress was being made and it gave me hope that I would start feeling better soon.

It helped so much to be able to let all of those bad experiences and negative times out on the table so I could finally start to address them. I had been dealing with so much death that I became numb to it and the more people passed away, the more broken and numb I began to feel inside. The grief from the loss of my grandfather was of course going to be the hardest pill to swallow, but the others weren't going to be easy either. In about a year and a half time span, I lost my Great-grandma Thelma, Uncle Buster, Aunt Barbara, Aunt Rhonda, Aunt Evie and my Grandfather, as well.

Losing those six people in that short span of time really took its toll on my mental health after a while. It started making me question life and its meaning because after losing so many people, I started feeling lost. It's like I had lost the whole older generation of my family in one year and none of it made sense to me. I was good at coming to terms with things and making sense of situations but death is something I've never been able to wrap my head around. Not that there's a proper way to grieve, but I'm sure the way I do it isn't healthy. Shelving the old memories and trying to hide my true feelings until I'm all alone is usually how I process the death of someone I love and it's not helpful at all.

Every time I turned around, I was attending another funeral and the obituaries started piling up around the house. Everywhere I looked it felt like I would see a picture of someone I lost and in those very moments, I would pretty much shut down for a while. After a while, the deaths of all of those people plus my grandmother's rapid decline in health proved to be too much for me to handle. Almost every day of my life, I spent at least a few hours at my grandparents' house. That's where all my friends were that I grew up with, and even where I got off the bus from school every day. I was there so often, that to this day I talk to people who believe I was living there.

Some people may not be able to relate to the pain because not everyone is fortunate to have a strong relationship with their grandparents, but I was blessed to have mine for all of my young life. They were an essential part of my upbringing and I went from seeing and talking to the both of them every day, to not being able to talk to either of them ever again in the blink of an eye. In about a year's time, other than my mother I had lost everyone in my life who had a hand in raising me.

After the appointment with Dr. Spencer was over, for the first time I was strongly considering taking medication for my depression. Talking about it so thoroughly with Dr. Spencer helped me form a different opinion about taking the medicine and the negative thoughts about what would happen to me started to go away. During my next appointment with Michelle, we talked about the general cycle the medicine takes you through so I wouldn't be caught by surprise by any of the effects. One of the things that she told me stuck out more than the others. She told me that the medicine would cause my emotions to go up and down a little bit and I would experience highs and lows at times. The first time I heard that alarmed me because the last thing I needed was something that caused a dip in my emotions. I had to look at the positive side of the situation and focus on when she said the medicine will change my mood overall and allow me to finally start to fight those negative thoughts. She told me that initially, I would feel a positive change in my mood and I would see an increase in my attitude after a few weeks when the medicine got a chance to build up in my system. She also warned me that after the first boost, the medicine might also cause me to experience one of those low, depressive mood swings and my energy would take a decrease for a while. Basically, for the first few trial weeks of the medication, there is a possibility that you'll experience some mood changes. Being depressed is like being sad all the time so what the medicine does at first is give your mind a second option from being depressed. Instead of all those negative thoughts, the medicine does something scientifically that helps balance out those thoughts and make it possible for you to enjoy yourself again. I was nervous about the downsides to the meds, since I didn't want them to make me even more depressed, but it became a risk I was willing to take.

When I finally went to go get the medication I was unexpectedly ready to start the new chapter of my life. I still had mixed emotions about it, but I was somewhat excited because of the possibility that the meds would help me feel better. The first time I took the medicine, it felt like a huge weight had been lifted off my shoulders. For the first time during this experience, I felt like I was finally making progress. This whole time, people have been telling me how important it was to start taking an antidepressant and I wasn't hearing any of it. After months of most people around me strongly suggesting I go down that road, I decided that taking the meds was the best option for me. Everyone around me also suggested I go to therapy and I was doing that so I felt like I was doing everything I could to finally defeat this depression. It felt like I had all hands-on deck and multiple plans in action so it would only be a matter of time before I started feeling better. I would say it was about a week later when my mood started positively changing. I started getting out of bed feeling a little bit happier and more motivated all of a sudden. The struggle of getting out of bed and finding motivation to do anything for the day started getting less and less taxing for me. My main dilemma now was all in my head. My own thinking was starting to side track me a little bit. I was wondering if the medicine was actually working or was it all in my head. I knew how badly I and everyone else wanted the medicine to work so I started thinking maybe it was all in my head. I mean, if you really set your mind to something, you can convince yourself of anything and I wasn't sure what was behind my recent mood changes. Was it the medicine, or did I just want to feel better so badly that I was telling myself I felt better? Only time would tell and being happier than I had been for months was enough for me at the time.

Chapter 20
My Support System

"Social support is a vital and effective part of depression recovery. It can turn around damaging isolation, affect a person's life focus, and generate solutions for depression management." – Erika Krull, MSEd LMHP, "Social Support Is Critical for Depression Recovery." Psychcentral.com

When I came home from the hospital, the first place I thought of was my boy Will's house. After the long episode, I went through with the cutting, I wanted to be out of the hospital, but I didn't want to specifically be at my house. For some reason I can't really explain, at one point I did whatever I could to stay away from my house. No matter what was going on, I would only go there if I absolutely had to. I had a few bags filled with clothes and shoes so I had enough stuff to last me for a couple weeks if I was able to avoid being home for that long.

Will is someone I've known since I was a baby. I consider him like a brother. We both grew up in the same neighborhood and our families have been close for decades. My house is like his house and vice versa so when I felt like I couldn't be home, Will's house was first on my list. When I left the hospital that night, that's exactly where I went. That's where I stayed consistently for about a month. For the first time in all our lives, whether Will was home or not, I was at his house. It was one of the only places I could go at the time where I was free of anxiety and pressure. When I was home, I felt like I was always supposed to be doing something whether it was working or going to school.

The worst part about it was that my depression was making it very difficult to do either one of those things so being home brought up conversations that I wasn't yet ready to have, and choices I wasn't yet ready to make. Being at Will's house afforded me time to relax and not worry about the things I couldn't handle at the moment. Even though I was able to find a place where I felt comfortable and safe, there's no way I could've been able to maintain without my great supporting cast. One of the main symptoms of depression is feeling alone, and I always had people around me that wouldn't allow me to feel alone no matter how stubborn I got. People who are depressed will push you away countless times and tell you that they're okay, but it's your job as a loved one to be able to see the signs and judge for yourself. Besides my family, I have a group of people that I consider my brothers and I look at them like we literally all share the same parents. They are an irreplaceable part of my support system.

All of our parents treat each of us like their own children and it creates a huge family environment for us all. Friends of mine from birth, in addition to friends from elementary and high school makes up this group of brothers. Being at Will's house felt like being home to me because his family is my family as well. You never get the sense that you're an outsider or not a part of the family when you have the kind of team I have around me. In order to make it through something as devastating as depression, you have to have a strong foundation around you to help push you forward.

Sometimes I felt like I was at Will's house too often, so I stayed with a set of twins in Brookline that I consider blood brothers of mine, Devon and Dashawn. I feel like I can call the twins anytime for anything. When I'm at their house, I am completely able to relax. We're used to just sitting around and playing video games and watching sports so that's what we did all day when I was with them. It allowed me to take my mind off of everything I was going through at the moment. The depression had to take a back seat anytime I was with any of my brothers. There was never any room for sadness or misery while they were around, they wouldn't allow it. It's very easy to be around someone and be there for them when everything's going great, and that person can support you as much as you support them, but you realize who your true friends are, when you see who sticks around when you have nothing to give back in that moment.

I have a very tight bond with each person in my circle and although we all have our differences, that bond never changes. One reason is because of the way we take care of each other. With my tight circle, I always feel like I have someone in my corner no matter what. Not just one person, but multiple people that will be there in the drop of a dime and I would do the exact same for them. We all go through out trials and tribulations and supporting each other can mean different things at different times. Sometimes it may mean staying at someone else's house for a few nights while you're able to get yourself together, or sometimes maybe even a two-hour phone call to settle your nerves. I have a person that can help me for every different situation I go through, and it feels like I have the ultimate safety-net behind me.

A few of my closest friends go to UMass Dartmouth where I went, but the others are pretty scattered around. The other keys to my circle include Jerome, Obi, Oshun, and my blood brother, Darius who all do various things. Obi and I have been friends since the second grade and our friendship has done nothing but grow into a brotherhood ever since. We gained an even bigger bond when we found out that we were both interested in playing basketball so that brought us even closer together. Now he studies engineering at Worcester Polytechnic Institute (WPI). His house is also somewhere I can go and feel like I am safe and around family. Over the years, his family has become my family and vice versa. He's someone, just like the rest of my circle that I can call anytime and he'll answer and help me with whatever I'm going through the best way he can. Darius who is my blood brother is someone I can't say enough about. He is like my backbone, he keeps me going and gives me confidence every day I wake up. Whenever I'm not feeling it and he knows it, he somehow always figures out a way to make me feel better and more confident about myself. He and I share a bond that can never be broken and we always have each other's back in any situation, despite what's going on.

Oshun is the newest member of my circle but I'm sure if you see us together, you wouldn't believe that was the case. He's the life of every party and always brings life to any situation he's involved in. I know whenever I'm down and get into one of my really depressive moods, I can count on Oshun to drag me out of the mud. We are together almost every day because he works in construction and his work site is basically around the corner from where I work. He's not only someone I consider a brother, but also a business partner and we have multiple business that we are currently working on together. Jerome is another one of my brothers and I've known him since the second grade as well, when I first started school in Brookline. We had so much in common when we first met and figured out we had even more in common as we got older that it was only right for us to be as close as we are. Jerome, like me is an entrepreneur, and he makes himself available so when I'm down I can call him and we will literally have hour-long conversations that help me tremendously. For me, calling Jerome is like having an on-the- phone therapy session. He gives whatever I need, whether it's just to sit and let me vent, or give me sound advice on what's going on in my life. We know each other so well that he can literally help me with anything I have going on because he has insight on most of my life. Whenever we get together and hang out, even if it's been a long time, it feels like we just were together the other day because of how strong that bond is. Rounding out my team of 'Bros" is Aaron who, to this day, is the one who pushes me to set and achieve my goals, and never lets me give up completely. He's the brother who, even in the midst of my darkest moods, never lets me feel sorry for myself for long.

While I was staying at Will's house, I was thinking about how I was going to start taking new steps in the right direction. Therapy with Michelle was still a great start, and key to my healing plan. She was extremely supportive through everything, and never gave up on me, even when I was avoiding her and missing appointments. She too, is a very important member of my support system, but I knew that I was going to need to do more.

Chapter 21
Looking Back

"Early life stress appears to radically alter neurobiological systems involved in the pathophysiology of depression... Far from being transient, stress experienced early in life has long-term effects on the entire body." - Erika Hatva, Childhood Trauma and Depression, Association of Psychological Science Observer July/August 2010

One day, my mom and I were doing some deep thinking and trying to figure out when I first started suffering from depression. We tried to think of changes I was making as a person that would usually recognize as abnormal for me. After a while of reminiscing about some of the main events in my life, we came to an interesting conclusion. Even though I had just recently been officially diagnosed with depression, I was suffering it for a lot longer than that. My mom and I started remembering some moments beginning in middle school when it seemed that my depression started to emerge.

For one thing, I started wearing hats and hoodies everywhere I went. It wasn't something I really thought about at the time, but thinking about it now, it was because I had lost a lot of my confidence. One feeling depression will give you is a sense of vulnerability. For no reason at all, you can feel completely exposed, like everyone is watching you and paying negative attention to your every move. It makes you feel like you're constantly being judged and it forces you to want to hide from everyone. That feeling caused me to start wearing hats and hoods everywhere because I used them as shields for myself. They gave me a sense of comfort that I didn't even realize I had lost. No matter how hot it was or what I was doing, I felt like I needed to have my shield on. No matter how much I loved basketball and having a hat or hood on not only affected my game (Not too much though) but also made me look weird, I wouldn't feel like me without one. They made me feel like even if people were looking, they couldn't fully see me. I would be shielded by whatever it was I had on my head and having the shield made me feel like myself again.

At this time, I was starting to feel the effects of depression and I had no idea. Looking back at it now, it's easy for me to see what I was doing at that age and see that there was a problem and I wish I would've caught it back then, but how was I supposed to? Given the fact that depression is almost never the topic of conversation, even at school, how was I supposed to know that I was starting to slip? I was being affected by the symptoms of depression but at the time, I couldn't match those symptoms with anything because depression almost seemed like it wasn't an option.

Once in a while, something dramatic may happen and the school will decide to have a day or so where they focus on depression and suicide prevention. Usually it's following a tragic event or something of that sort so it's more of a debrief of the situation that happened. Those lectures usually just consist of a few teachers and faculty members telling you that you have their full support and that it's important to reach out if you feel like you're going to hurt yourself. To me, the whole thing is more like a protocol situation. It's one of those things that the school feels like they have to do rather than something they really wanted to touch on. If that were the case, there would be a lot more focus in school about mental illness. Not that the other material being taught in school isn't important, but how are you supposed to thrive in school if you're depressed? More importantly, how are you supposed to help cure this depression if you don't even know you have it? It's a cycle that keeps coming back to society needing to be better informed about what's going on with depression. If schools took the time to maybe implement a class once or twice a week that puts emphasis on self-awareness and describing what having depression looked like, we'd be dealing with fewer cases. If you have depression and you don't know it, it can take a huge toll on how you feel about yourself. You start to dislike things you normally like, have a lot less patience and tolerance, and become way more irritable than usual. Dealing with all that while being in school is like fighting multiple wars at once. Not only do you have to deal with the natural stresses that school brings, but also now you have to make sure you put on your poker face so no one knows what you're going through.

Nowadays, something that most people are afraid of is being different than the "average person". People who have depression and suffer from the symptoms I discussed often feel alone because they feel like they're the only one going through it. If people were more aware of how prevalent depression is and realized that it's a perfectly normal struggle to go through, we would have a lot more people coming forward about how they feel. I think it's vital that we start teaching kids at a young age that it's okay to tell someone when you're feeling sad. It becomes normal for everyone to keep their emotions bottled up if that's what they've been doing their whole lives.

Have you ever looked at the cuts on someone's wrist and immediately asked them if they needed help? I highly doubt it, because that's weird, right? Up until this year, I certainly used to think so. Late in middle school and all throughout high school I would notice a few people who had cuts on their arms. I can remember each time because it never failed to give me the same feeling. All of a sudden, my mind would go somewhere and I would get lost. A million questions would circle around my head and of course the biggest one of all was why? Over and over I would just ask myself what that person could possibly be going through in order to get to that point. At the same time, I would also think about how I would never do that to myself. It was something that somewhat consumed me because I couldn't figure it out to save my life and I didn't want to ask anyone else about it either. It was a weird thing to go home and talk to your parents or guardians about because I'm sure they'd follow up with a million questions on why you're asking that question. I was so strong-minded and I told myself over and over that no matter what was going in on my life, I would refrain from hurting myself. I always wanted to ask those people what was happening that was so bad. Maybe I could help, or just listen, but it was too much. At those times, I was either sitting in class or walking in the hallways and even though asking if they needed help constantly crossed my mind, I was afraid to say anything. I didn't want to seem like a pest and bother them about it, especially while there were other people around. I also had no idea how to approach the situation, if I did talk to them, what would I even say? What could I possibly have to offer that could help this person out?

I'm sure that's what most people think when they come across that particular situation. Little do you know, anything at all can go a long way. When I hit my rock bottom, I realized exactly what it was those people were going through. Every day I was struggling with the ideas that no one loved or cared about me and nothing was ever going to get better. Once you fall into that cycle of negative thinking, it's unimaginably hard to get out of it. It becomes a downward spiral of horrible thoughts and ideas that you end up convincing yourself are true. During my low points, I was feeling like no matter how much I expressed myself and everyone was starting to realize what I was going through, no one understood me. No one knew the severity of my depression and it started to anger me. With all the emotions I was already fighting, anger was the last one I needed. It made me bitter towards most of the people around me because I started feeling like they didn't care. I wasn't getting any better, as a matter of fact worse, and no one was doing anything about it. I totally convinced myself that the reality was I was by myself and it was me against the world. I was going to have to fight this depression by myself and I had no clue how.

Chapter 22
Looking Forward: The Road to Recovery

"I will not give up on life again. There's so many people that will never get the chance to have their voice heard… I do it for them." – Kanye West, Award winning rap artist

With the medicine and the therapy working together now, I continued working for my mom at Smart from the Start and she allowed me to have flexible hours that fit how I was feeling. Smart from the Start is honestly like one of my mother's babies. She founded the organization which has as its mission to provide early education and family support services to families with little children, living in very low-income communities in Boston and Washington, DC. My siblings and I started volunteering 10 years ago, when Smart first began programming and it's been a part of our lives ever since. Having a job gave me something to wake up for each morning, and helped raise my motivation. It also put money in my pocket. Having money is always something that's constantly on my mind so now that I had a stable income, there was one less thing in that depression backpack I was carrying around.

Although there were more positives than negatives when it came to having a job again, some of the negatives were particularly difficult to deal with. Things that came easy to me before the depression were a lot harder. One of things was engaging in everyday interaction with staff members. Under normal circumstances, I'm a very outgoing person who's never shy, who enjoys laughing and talking with others and always have something to say. The depression took a lot of that away from me so going to work and having to actually communicate with people was hard for me. Also, having to deal with real-life issues at work, like the everyday office gossip and things of that nature caused me to go backward a few times in terms of my progress. Even though it was tough to be at work at times, I fought hard to force myself to keep pushing. Staying positive and happy in spite of the rumors and gossip swirling around wasn't easy, but with the tools I was mastering in therapy and the medicine working its way into my system, my battle with depression and the rippling effects was getting a little bit easier.

After a few weeks of taking the medicine consistently and also going to therapy, my mood took a huge dip. I remembered Michelle telling me that there was a chance I'd experience a drop in my mood due to the possible ups and downs the medicine sends you on at first but I didn't expect it to hit me the way it did. A lot of feelings depression gives you are impossible to describe but this feeling just completely wiped me out. After a couple weeks of feeling better, I had crashed again. All of a sudden, I was hit with this bout of sadness and I wanted to give up on everything. This time, not only was I sad, but I was angry. I was angry with everyone that had tried to convince me to take meds or go to therapy because I felt like they didn't work. I started to hate therapy and eventually stopped going. The depression was making me feel like nothing was working so everything I was doing was a waste of time. I immediately wanted to stop taking the medicine but I knew it wasn't healthy for me to just stop all of a sudden. I told myself that therapy was useless and there was no point in going back because after all this time, I was still depressed. This mindset had me ready to give up on everything and everybody and I felt like I was back at square one. I didn't know why I was feeling this way. In my opinion I was doing everything I was supposed to do, why was I back to where I started?

While I was going through this tough time of misunderstanding and sadness, I remembered back to the conversation I had with Michelle and started thinking about

112

how she told me I would experience a crash sooner or later. Having that knowledge in the back of my head helped me a little bit but going through that stretch was tough. I was taking the medicine the way I was supposed to everyday, but I stopped feeling better all of a sudden. It caused me to start second-guessing the medicine and whether it ever really worked or if it was all in my head because I wanted it to work so badly. The thought of me taking this big step and taking the medicine only for it to not work started making me feel like taking the medicine was useless. I battled back and forth in my head about whether or not I wanted to keep taking the meds. After a few days of thinking hard but still not feeling better, I decided that I was going to stop taking the medicine. The mental hurdle of taking the medicine in the first place was tough for me, so if it wasn't going to work I saw no need in continuing to live outside of my comfort zone for it. I told a few people around me like my mom and a couple of close friends and of course they all had the same response. It had only been a few days since I stopped taking the meds, but I knew in the back of my head that it wasn't healthy for me to just stop taking the meds all of a sudden. That is an issue that everyone who I told stressed to me as well. I was just so aggravated and disappointed that I was experiencing such a low feeling while I was on the meds that it made me resentful towards them. What some people started telling me was that instead of not taking the medicine, I should just get an increase in my dosage. For some reason, I hadn't thought of that idea before. Now I had to have another long conversation with myself about what I was going to do next. The hardest part here for me was taking the meds in the first place; now I had to consider taking even more of what I had so it could really work. It was less than a week that I had stopped taking the medicine and overall, I started feeling worse. The medicine was at least doing a good job of stabilizing my mood and allowing myself to control whether I was happy or sad, not just waking up sad like usual and without it, I was just down all the time. After weighing the options, I had (which were basically to feel better or not) I decided that I was going to increase my dosage of meds.

At this point, it felt like all I could do was hope, hope that increasing my dosage of Prozac would be the solution to my most recent setback. It made me anxious because everything was out of my hands and there wasn't much I could do to control what was going on with me. I had to just wait and be patient until the medication started working. After consistently being in a bad slump for about a week or so, I started gaining more motivation to get up. It's a hard concept to explain but when you're depressed you can allow the depression to defeat you so much that you can't get out of bed if you tried. After a few days of increasing my meds, I found it easier to find reasons to get up. Before I laid in bed and found reasons to stay in bed. It could be any small thing that I could think up and I convinced myself that it was enough to keep me in the house for the day. Finally, my thought process started becoming a bit more positive. Those negative thoughts weren't so prominent and my energy and motivation levels started to rise. I started gaining some of my confidence back and started to want to do things again like wanting to eat again. During the course of my depression, I managed to lose about thirty pounds because my appetite had gone away completely. I was down to about one meal per day and usually that wasn't even a full meal. I could go a full day on snacks and blue Powerade drinks, and most of the time that's exactly what I did. After I increased my medication and took it on a regular basis, eating meals started becoming a priority again. Before the meds, I tended to skip meals, because simply deciding what I was going to eat, and preparing meals was too stressful. I didn't feel like getting up to make anything and the foods that I used to love, I just didn't care for anymore.

All of a sudden, in the mornings instead of going right into my routine of going to work, I would stop and grab breakfast. Before, food wasn't even on my list of things to do during the day. It was more something that I would do if the opportunity presented itself and usually I made sure it didn't. I was feeling like I did when I first originally started the Prozac. My everyday mood was better and it got easier for me to eliminate and ignore the bad thoughts that would constantly try to take over. With the change in my mood, I started going to work on a consistent basis, eating more regularly, and I felt a lot more comfortable being alone. I started going home more because after a while it became somewhere I actually wanted to be and the negative things about it didn't outweigh the positives of having a home base. The medicine was doing exactly what everyone was saying it was going to do. It helped balance my thoughts so the negative wasn't such a reality and I was able to start thinking more positively. For months, I found it hard to find the good in anything but all of a sudden, life started to become more fun.

With the increase in my medicine, I felt like I had a lot more control of my life. For months now, depression had stripped away my independence and became a part of me. It controlled my mental health so much that it destroyed my ability to do almost anything physically and completely wiped away my motivation. I didn't care what tomorrow would bring, or if tomorrow even came at all. I didn't want to eat anything and I was starting to lose more and more weight each day. I felt lost and seriously didn't see a solution or end to this nightmare I was living. Everyone was telling me how much the medicine and the therapy worked, especially when they work together but for so long I didn't want to hear it. In my mind, I couldn't wrap my head around the idea that either one of those solutions would help me. How in the hell will talking to a stranger help my depression? I asked myself that over and over and told myself that it wouldn't work so I would shoot the idea down every time it was brought up. The medicine on the other hand seemed like something I would never even give much thought to. I would talk about the side effects because they did worry me a little bit but for the most part, nothing drove me further away from taking meds more than that feeling, that stigma that comes with taking medicine.

Taking medicine for something going on in your head seemed like a foreign concept to me, mostly because I didn't understand how this medicine would change the way I thought and help cure my depression in any way. Now after about a month of constantly taking the medicine and going to my therapy appointments, I started feeling like I had life once again. I had more control of what was going on in my head and the positives of life were slowly creeping their way back into my thought process. I was amazed at the progress I was making due to these two options that I was so against at the beginning. I was feeling more like myself again and went back to a normal schedule. Instead of waking up at random times and ultimately deciding that I was going to just stay in the house all day, I set up a consistent work schedule and stuck to it for the most part. I still have my days where I wake up and feel pretty down but I don't allow it to keep me in the house anymore. Those negative thoughts aren't so strong anymore so it is easier for me to push them in the back of my head and start to think about things that are more realistic, like the fact that there's potential to have a great day. I didn't see that potential for a long time and that's what made it so easy to stay in. I was afraid of the real world, so it became scary to me and it made me stagnant in life. I was scared of what was going to happen in the next chapter so I didn't want to turn the page. Now I am excited to get up, go to work in the morning, and grab breakfast on the way. For months, I had to be around certain people in order to feel even a little bit comfortable wherever I was but now, the environment doesn't matter so much. I am not letting everyone and everything else (including the depression) derail what I planned for that day. I can feel my self-esteem coming back and growing by the day as well. Some people have even started telling me that they could tell the difference by the way I carry myself. I don't have to tell anyone that I was feeling better; they can see it all over my face. Now I don't have that sad, defeated look on my face all the time, that smile is back and it is genuine. I don't have to put on a poker face for people anymore because there is true happiness inside now. I am starting to make plans again and giving myself more and more to do in order to stay busy. The Prozac alone is doing great for me, but I still suffer from mood changes at times so I went in to talk to my doctor about them. I have been a lot happier than before on a regular basis but my mood wasn't exactly as stable as I wanted it to be. Sometimes I would still get really down all of a sudden and I knew the depression wasn't gone but I wanted to see if there was another solution for the mood changes. My doctor told me that what I was experiencing was normal, and she suggested that I take something that is intended to stabilize my mood. The medicine is called Abilify and it is also used to help treat depression and stabilize your mood. So now I went from not taking anything and not seeing anyone, to seeing two doctors for therapy and taking Prozac and Abilify for my depression. I am being pretty proactive now in trying to get over this horrible illness. The Abilify was different from the other meds out there because it doesn't take as long as the others to start working. Now I am taking both meds at the same time, and feel as good as I felt since this all started.

Now that I have done everything I felt like I could to start feeling better and all the options are working, I am ready to start a new venture. One of the ideas a few people gave me along the way during my journey through depression was that I could start writing in a journal and recording what I went through. At the time, I didn't give much thought to it. I'm not sure why but it didn't seem like something I may enjoy doing. Now, after everything that has happened and me feeling a lot better, I decided that I was going to start writing about my trials and tribulations with depression. At first, I had no idea what I was going to do with it. Lots of people told me that I was a good writer during middle school and high school, but I never wrote anything I didn't have to. If it wasn't for school or work, you would never catch me writing or typing about anything. This experience though was a lot different. This was about me and what my life has been like for the past year. I had done things I never thought I'd do, seen things I never thought I'd see, and was starting to make it through something I thought was going to be the end of me.

My whole perspective on life changed and I wanted to share my story with anyone who took the time to read it. At first, I was just going to write a big journal and take it from there, but before I even started typing I decided that if I was going to do this than I was going to go all the way. Right then and there I decided that I was going to turn this project into a published book. I was nervous about letting everyone I knew as well as plenty of strangers reading so much about me, but after a few days I decided that the positives of publishing a book like this completely outweighed the negatives. My focus than shifted away from myself and I started thinking about what the book could do for other people. The stigma of having depression can be so strong that most people don't even let anyone know they're suffering from it. I wanted to create this book so that people can see where I was when this whole thing started and that I was in the same position as I'm sure millions of people are in right now while you read this. I wanted to create this book to reassure the people who suffer from depression that I understand. You can learn to cope with it, and it can get so much better. For a while I didn't see any way that this illness was going to go away by talking to some therapist or even by taking medicine, but once I got past being stubborn and worrying about those stigmas, I was able to dedicate myself to getting better.

I understand exactly how hard it is to tell people you have depression first and foremost, but I'm here to let everyone know who suffers from depression that it's okay to let people in your life help you. The ones you love won't judge you and there are solutions for depression. It's also very important for people around those who suffer from depression to be supportive in the best ways possible. Those of us who have depression can oftentimes be very difficult to reach but it's vital for you to stick by us in our toughest times. As I talked about earlier, having a great support system can literally make or break anyone's fight with depression. Depression can make you feel like your life is over and that it may even be time to end it, but take it from me, depression doesn't have to define you. After the initial shocker of being diagnosed with depression, don't wait to get better like I did, attack depression head on. It's a scary illness to go through because it involves your mental state and you think nobody else can possibly understand what you're going through. However, the truth is there are millions of people around the world fighting the exact same battle, and hopefully after reading my story, you will have better insight and an array of new weapons, so that you battle will be won and you will, be able to help others, too.

Made in the USA
Middletown, DE
22 October 2021